CASSELL'S GARDEN DIRECTORIES

Water Gardens

CASSELL'S GARDEN DIRECTORIES

Water Gardens

EVERYTHING YOU NEED TO CREATE A GARDEN

RICHARD BIRD

Consultant Editor
LUCY HUNTINGTON

CASSELL&CO

First published in the United Kingdom in 2002 by CASSELL & CO.

Design and text copyright © The Ivy Press Limited 2000

The moral right of Richard Bird to be identified as the author of this work has been
asserted in accordance with the Copyright, Designs and Patents Act of 1988.

A CIP Catalogue record for this book
is available from the British Library

ISBN 0 304 36234 4

This book was conceived,
designed and produced by
THE IVY PRESS LIMITED
The Old Candlemakers, West Street,
Lewes, East Sussex BN7 2NZ

Creative Director: PETER BRIDGEWATER
Designers: AXIS DESIGN
Editorial Director: SOPHIE COLLINS
Project Editor: ANDREW KIRK
Editor: CLAIRE MUSTERS
Illustrations: VANESSA LUFF & PETER BULL
Picture Researcher: LIZ EDDISON

Originated and printed in China by
Hong Kong Graphics and Printing Ltd

This book is typeset in 10.5/13 Linotype Perpetua and Univers

CASSELL & CO.
Wellington House, 125 Strand, London WC2R 0BB

CONTENTS

INTRODUCTION

Water has a magnetism, whether it be the sea, a lake or a simple pond. In a garden, of course, any water feature has usually been artificially created, but it still attracts the eye and the ear. Most people find it almost impossible not to linger by a garden pool. There is no doubt that water can add a different dimension to a garden, however small. There is a huge variety of ways of using water in the garden, and a wide choice in the way that plants can be used to enhance the whole effect.

Gardeners who have natural water in their garden – a stream or a pond that was there before the garden was made, rather than one built with a plastic liner of some sort – are the lucky ones. Such gardens are few and far between today. The secret of good water gardening is to use all the gardener's means to make artificial water features, where a pond or stream has had to be constructed, look as natural as possible. This involves clever use of the plants as well as the design of the feature itself. There are, of course, water features that do not have any plants in them at all, but we are concentrating on those that are planted.

FEATURING WATER

The water garden may form the focal point of a garden; if so, visitors will make a beeline for it ignoring other attractions. It does not have to be in the centre of the garden, however – it can be tucked away to be stumbled

THEN AND NOW

❧ Down the ages water has played a vital part not only in the design of gardens, but also a role in the way gardens have been used, that is to say, for relaxation.
❧ In the past the water itself was the prime attraction of the water garden, and was often used in formal patterns. Now it is used in a more informal way and planting plays a much more important role.

on as a pleasant surprise. Some ponds fit into the garden as if they have always been there. These 'comfortable' ponds are perfect for accompanying informal areas. The water garden can take a number of different forms, from ponds and pools to streams, runnels, spouts, fountains and waterfalls. There may be deep water in the middle of ponds, and shallow water at the edges or margins. It may be a bog garden, where the soil is kept moist rather than constantly under deep water. The area beside a stream, waterfall or fountain is also a good place for moisture-loving plants to grow – the spray from the splashing water provides just the right amount of dampness for them.

WATER PLANTS

The lure of such gardens is mainly the water, but this is enhanced by the beauty of the plants associated with it. In water, it is the movement, reflections and sound that combine to form its attraction. Plants are often the subject of the water's reflections; they catch the light and are

LEFT *A tiny water feature, such as this delightful fountain set in an ornamental container, can bring the welcome sight and sound of water into even the smallest garden.*

constantly affected by the subtle movement of the water. Plants help keep the water clear and free of algae, as well as supporting the wildlife that lives within and around it.

The number of attractive plants that grow either in water or in very wet conditions is relatively small. There are, however, many plants that thrive in moist conditions. These may well be woodland plants that cannot survive in the open sun unless there is plenty of moisture for their roots to take up. Hostas and hemerocallis, for example, fall into this group. There are other plants that, although they do not really like moist conditions, nonetheless look particularly good when associated with water. *Betula pendula* (silver birch), for example, prefers a free-draining soil, but looks magnificent when reflected in water. It is fortunate for gardeners that this latter group exists, as the area around ponds is often very dry. This is because the liner prevents the water from the pond mixing with the surrounding soil. This means that the edge near a pond is therefore perfect for such plants.

ABOVE *If you have the room, the water garden can be made as elaborate as you like. This* *one incorporates water spouts, rocks and lush planting, giving a spectacular overall effect.*

SIGHT AND SOUND

The visual aspect of water is not the only consideration you should have in mind when planning a water garden – sound is very important, too. This is usually associated with the movement of water, such as in a fountain or cascade, but it can also be created by the wind blowing through the plants that are growing around the margins of a pool, particularly in winter when the wind vibrates the dried remains of rushes. The sight and sound associated with water have a very calming effect. It makes an ideal feature in a garden where people want to relax. Sitting beside a pool or stream after a long hard day can help the body and mind in a way that few other things can. In this book we will look at the water garden it all its forms, with an emphasis on the planting associated with them.

HOW TO USE THIS BOOK

Cassell's Garden Directories have been conceived and written to appeal both to gardening beginners and to confident gardeners who need advice for a specific project. Each book focuses on a particular type of garden, drawing on the experience of an established expert. The emphasis of each book is on a practical and down-to-earth approach that takes into account the space, time and money that you have available. The ideas and techniques in these books will help you to produce an attractive and manageable garden that you will enjoy and relax in for many years to come.

Water Gardens demystifies the whole area of water gardening, revealing that anyone can have a relaxing, peaceful water feature as part of their garden, and that it really is simple to create one. The book is divided into three sections. The opening section, Planning a Water Garden, introduces the subject of water gardens and plants, looking at the different kinds of effects that can be achieved and the range of water plants that is available. There are also three inspirational garden plans covering very different types of water features.

Part Two of the book, Creating a Water Garden, moves on to the practicalities of selecting, buying and propagating water plants. This section opens with advice on the range of different features that can make up a water garden, such as edgings for a pond, types of fountains and fish. The remainder of Part Two is packed with practical information on basic techniques, such as how to plant water plants in different water depths and the appropriate aftercare and

maintenance. Moving on from this basic grounding, this section then encourages you to put your skills to work with a series of specific projects such as creating a miniature pond, a half-barrel pool, for example, or making and planting a bog garden. Step-by-step illustrations throughout this section show clearly and simply what you need to do to achieve the best results. Also included are handy hints and tips, points to watch out for, and star plants that are particularly suitable for the projects described.

The final part of the book, The Plant Directory, is a comprehensive listing of all the plants mentioned in the earlier sections, together with other plants that you can place in a water feature. It includes submerged, floating, deep-water, marginal and bog plants as well as shrubs, trees, grasses and bamboos that work well beside water features. Each plant is illustrated, and there is complete information about the required growing conditions, speed of growth and ease of maintenance.

GARDEN SCHEMES are included to inspire ou when creating your own garden.

COLOUR PHOTOGRAPHS show what can be achieved with a little effort and imagination.

3D PLANS show the best planting scheme to enable you to achieve the desired effect.

THE KEY FEATURES of each plant used are described to help you visualize the plan.

CHOICES SPREADS show a selection of water features, plants and different edgings that might be appropriate in your water garden.

THE CHECKLIST details important things to look out for in choosing garden features.

PRACTICAL SPREADS give useful information on basic techniques and garden projects.

CLEAR ILLUSTRATIONS show each step of the process.

THE PLANT DIRECTORY is organized into categories making it simple to find a particular type of plant..

COLOUR PHOTOGRAPHS clearly identify each plant listed.

COLOUR PHOTOGRAPHS help you to decide on the appropriate feature for your garden.

EXPLANATORY TEXT describes the various possibilities available in each category.

WATCHPOINTS BOXES give a checklist of cautions and problems to look out for.

CLEAR DESCRIPTIVE TEXT details the appearance and the appropriate growing conditions for each plant.

THE SYMBOLS PANEL gives important information on features such as speed of growth and shade tolerance.

SIDEBAR shows at a glance the season of interest for each plant.

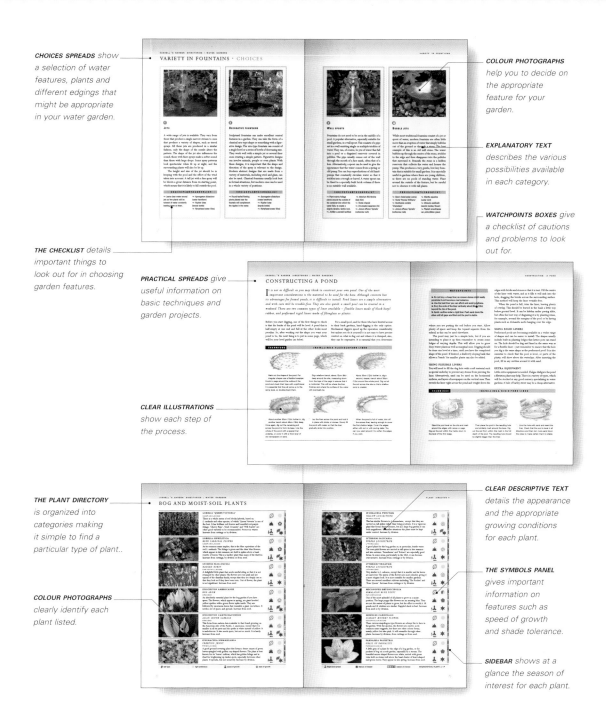

1

PLANNING A WATER GARDEN

When planning a water feature and its associated planting, it is best to have a clear idea of your aims, since such a feature is likely to be permanent and will not be easy to change once finished. Making a rough plan will help to identify how the water feature will look, what kind of planting will provide the right balance, and whether it will fit in with the rest of the garden. This chapter explores all these considerations, and includes a variety of plans to give you inspiration for your own garden.

LEFT *The designer of this water feature clearly intended to evoke a mood of quiet reflection, using lighting to enhance the effect.*

WHY HAVE A WATER GARDEN?

Water is a source of fascination for most people. It can display a variety of moods — from soothing tranquillity to bubbling excitement. Still water offers shimmering reflections, and moving water adds sound and activity to the equation. Plants that thrive in water, or near to it, have a lushness not often matched in the rest of the garden. Remember, however, that water can also be a danger, especially for children, who love playing with it — safety is of paramount importance, always make sure children are watched when they are near water.

In the rush of the modern world, still water plays a very important role as a calming influence. It is frequently added to office blocks, city centres and other busy places to provide just this effect. In the garden, where other calming influences are already at work, its role is magnified. To sit or stand near a pool of water amid green vegetation and colourful flowers can be a wonderful antidote to the busy world beyond the garden boundaries.

Still water is like a mirror, and it will reflect all that stands above it. This silent reflection has a peaceful effect on the garden and those that use it. It also enhances the look of surrounding plants by reflecting light onto them. This quality can very easily be exploited by the gardener when choosing plants — think about how their shapes will be reflected in the water, and how the use of the reflected light will affect their overall appearance.

POINTS TO CONSIDER

❧ Water can bring peace and tranquillity to your garden to help you relax and unwind.

❧ It is fascinating to watch water, as there is constant movement, even if it is just ripples caused by the breeze. Water also attracts wildlife into the garden to drink and bathe.

❧ If you want to increase the range of plants in your garden, a water garden will enable you to grow plants that would not survive in other parts of the garden.

COOLNESS AND MOISTURE

Part of the feeling of calm generated by a water feature is as result of the coolness it creates. Just looking at water makes you feel cool, and trailing a hand in it physically cools you down. The sound of falling water from a fountain is also very refreshing, and the drops do actually cool the air as they pass through it. In a damp, shaded garden, a pool might add a bit too much extra moisture to the air, but in most gardens the evaporating water will add a welcome touch of humidity to the dry atmosphere. It will also provide much-needed moisture to the plants around the pond's margins.

SOUND AND MOVEMENT

Water is rarely dull. Whereas a lawn is just an expanse of green, a sheet of water is usually doing something. The slightest breeze can set it rippling, fish break the surface,

LEFT *The sound of splashing water can be soothing after a hard day. This can be given a touch of humour, such as that provided by these gargoyles spouting into a formal pool.*

fountains splash into it. There is always plenty to watch, even on rainy days you can get pleasure from water, watching the pattern of raindrops falling onto the surface.

Water on the move can be exciting, and streams, water-falls and cascades always ensure a lot of movement. Moving water creates sound – from the splashing of streams to the light patter of the fine drops from the spray of a fountain. Such sounds in a garden are particularly restful, and allow the mind to concentrate on calmer matters.

A PLACE FOR PLANTS

One of the big advantages of having a pond, or another water feature, as part of your garden design is that it creates a very special habitat for plants that cannot be grown in any other way. Some of these are plants that grow in deep water, with leaves and flowers floating on the surface. Others prefer the edges of a pool. There are also some that like the boggy conditions that occur next to a pond, either somewhere in its margins or in a specially created bog garden. A pond opens up a vast range of new plants for the gardener. Even a garden that only has a half-barrel of water can have a few choice plants added to it to increase interest. Some plants are not dependent on open water; water splashing onto pebbles from a spout will help create the right humid atmosphere for growing ferns, hostas and other lush foliage plants that will give the area nearby a cool feel. Whatever style and size of water garden you choose, a large part of the fun of creating it will lie in the selection and growing of water plants.

ABOVE *With a large pond, plants can provide the vital finishing touch. Cortaderia selloana (pampas grass) looks magnificent in this setting.*

TYPES OF WATER GARDEN

*A*s with any aspect of garden design, it is important to consider what kind of impact you want to create with your water garden. It should fit into the overall garden style, enhancing all the existing features. Sometimes circumstances may prevent you doing exactly what you would like to do, but there are usually other equally satisfying options. If you have young children, it is safer to use trickling spouts or bubble fountains rather than ponds.

One of the biggest choices is between a formal and an informal pool. Formal ones tend to work in isolation, and are often surrounded by paths or a patio. They are geometric in shape: a circle, a square, a rectangle or a hexagon. Whatever the shape of the pond, the edge is always well defined, giving the whole a crisp finish.

The planting in formal pools is usually very limited. It can be restricted to one or two groups of plants – a few irises in each corner, for example, or just a few water lilies. In larger ponds there may be several groups of plants, usually the same type planted at regular intervals. The plants rarely blur the shape of the pool. This style of pool suits more formal gardens, ones that are precisely ordered. A formal pool must be maintained regularly to ensure that the plants do not become too rampant, but this is easy to do and does not take up very much time.

Informal ponds can be a wide variety of shapes – they are often irregular and include sinuous lines. The edges or banks are not necessarily well defined. There might be a beach of pebbles sloping down into the water in one place and grassy banks in another. Even if the lines are more defined they are usually softened or even lost because of the plants growing beside them or hanging over them.

This type of pond has a mixture of types of plant, which often extend beyond the pool into an adjacent bog garden or a bank planted with normal garden plants. The surface of the pond is visible, but does not play such an important design role as in the formal garden. This kind of pond is well suited to the more casual garden, where the design is not rigid or formal. An informal pool will require much more attention than a formal one, as it has a lot more plants in it. However, the timing and frequency of this care is not as critical, since the plants are allowed to spread naturally.

LEFT *A formal pool has straight edges that are not hidden by trailing plants. It may be very stylized in both colour, such as this strong blue, and form, with striking shapes and designs.*

THE NATURAL POND

A natural pond is one that looks as though it could be in the country rather than part of a garden. It has an informal shape and plenty of vegetation growing in and around it. This creates a habitat that will attract wild creatures as well as being suitable for those animals, such as fish, that are deliberately placed in it. A truly natural pond does not have an artificial liner but is 'puddled' (lined) with clay. However, this is often impractical and many gardeners use either a butyl liner, or a cheaper polythene one, covered with a layer of clay or other heavy soil.

The key to a natural pond is the planting. Although garden plants can be used, it is often best to search out the native ones that would naturally grow in and around a pond. Stands of reeds and rushes often help to create this effect. However, be aware that many 'wild' plants are not very attractive and are frequently rampant – so in a garden situation, particularly a small one, it is advisable to use cultivated plants; but make sure you use them in such a way as to give the effect of a natural pond. Avoid plants that will completely cover the surface of the pond.

THEN AND NOW

🌢 There used to be many natural ponds in the countryside providing perfect habitats for wildlife. Now that these are decreasing, garden ponds are becoming valuable habitats.
🌢 Pools are now places for planting up, rather than simply the receptacles for reflecting or moving water that they often were in the past.

NON-POOL WATER FEATURES

Fountains and spouts create the sound and sight of moving water without taking up much space. The water can fall into basins, troughs or old sinks filled with pebbles. Such features can be planted to great effect and are the best way of creating a water garden in a limited space. Streams may already exist or can be constructed.

BELOW *An informal natural pond has planting that looks as if the scene has come straight out of the wild, whereas in reality a lot of planning and thought has been put into the design.*

TYPES OF WATER PLANT

*W*ater plants are different from other types of plant as the gardener purposely grows not only attractive varieties but also, for practical reasons, some that are not so pretty. These may lie completely below the water and never be seen — but they are needed to oxygenate the water. Once you move onto the banks and into the bog garden, visual qualities become important again, and plants are chosen accordingly.

Most water plants can be categorized by their position in or relative to the water. The number of plants is relatively low, although in some cases there are plenty of different cultivars to choose from. The groups defined below start from the middle of the pond and work outwards.

BELOW-SURFACE PLANTS

These plants are usually known as oxygenators (*see pages 18–19*). They are not particularly attractive; their prime function is to provide the water with oxygen. They tend to be rapid growers and need to be kept in check, by removing quantities of the plants so they do not choke the pond. They are extremely easy to propagate, but if you take pieces from other people's ponds make sure you are not bringing algae in with them.

BELOW *Marginal plants like hostas grow around the side of the pond, and can be used to soften and even hide its edges.*

DEEP-WATER PLANTS

These are plants, such as water lilies (*Nymphaea*), which have their roots in the bottom of the pond and their leaves and flowers floating on the surface. Most have large round or oval leaves, and in most cases these are attractive in their own right. It is the flowers, however, that have most appeal for water gardeners. Several are also sweetly scented and attract pollinators to travel over the water. They are not difficult to propagate, but need to be introduced to their final depth stage by stage so that they have time to extend.

FLOATING WATER PLANTS

Floating plants have leaves that float on the surface and roots that dangle just below, in the water rather than plunging down to the mud. They can colonize the whole surface of a pond in a short time, and as a result the water cannot be seen and plants below die through lack of light. Therefore they need to be thinned at regular intervals. Never throw discarded floating plants into natural streams

as they can soon choke a waterway. One of the most attractive, *Azolla filiculoides* (fairy moss), is also one of the worst offenders. These plants often look best in small ponds.

MARGINAL AND BOG PLANTS

Marginal plants provide most of the interest in a pond because they are planted around the edges, in shallow water, where they can be readily seen. They vary in leaf shape, and in the colour and shape of the flowers. They can disguise the edge of the pond, breaking possibly severe lines along the banks and hiding ugly liners. In the pond, they also provide plenty of shelter for its inhabitants.

The areas next to the pond where the soil is wet but not waterlogged are known as 'boggy'. There are not many true bog plants that are attractive enough to be grown in the garden, but there are plenty of other plants that like the moist conditions and help to create a very attractive planting. If the bog garden area is very wet then some of the marginals will also happily grow there.

ABOVE *In a very large pond, a huge raft of water lilies can look spectacular, especially when* *they are all in flower. It is important, however, to keep some areas of water clear.*

PLANTS FOR DRY BANKS

Plenty of plants that are not true water plants associate well with water, such as *Alchemilla mollis*. Some trees and bushes also look good growing on a dry bank next to water. Such plants play an important role in any water garden.

POINTS TO CONSIDER

- A balance between all the different types of plants is necessary to create a successful pond.
- The pond should be constructed with different depths of water to accommodate many different types of plant.
- If there is room for only one water feature in your garden, a bog garden can accommodate a greater diversity of plants than any of the other features.

GETTING THE BALANCE RIGHT

A water garden is a living community and, although you will need to impose certain controls over it, should be treated as a natural habitat. In a pond, in order for both plant and animal life to thrive, it is vital to achieve the correct balance between all the various elements it contains. This means keeping the water well oxygenated, and providing both food and shelter for fish and other wildlife, as well as maintaining an attractive visual balance between areas of open water and your chosen plantings.

There is always one group in a pond trying to dominate. The pondweeds or algae may be desperate to take over, there may be an excess of mosquito larvae or the fish may be becoming too numerous. If any one of these groups takes over the pond, the environment will become unbalanced. It is therefore essential to keep them all under control. You should, for example, have enough weed to provide oxygen, food and shelter, but not so much that it blocks the sun and fills the pond. The art of water gardening is to create and maintain a balanced environment.

OXYGENATORS

One of the first essentials in a pond is oxygen. Plants that release oxygen into the water, at the same time using up any excess carbon dioxide, are called oxygenators. These are submerged plants that grow mainly below the surface of the pond. They feed on the nutrients in the water and soil at the bottom of the pond and then release oxygen during daylight hours. The reduction of nutrients also helps to keep algae under control. Algae are a nuisance because not only do they make a pool look dreadful but they also block out the sun. The sun's rays are vital for plants and animals to remain healthy.

FOOD AND SHELTER

Plants can provide food and shelter for various creatures. They create areas for the young to hide from predators and they provide sites for dragonflies and others to deposit their eggs. Large-leaved floating plants also provide shade. Marginal plants act as a forest for the pond's inhabitants.

OPEN WATER VERSUS PLANTS

It is important to keep a balance between the number of plants in the pond and the amount of open water, both for visual reasons and to leave enough space for the living

LEFT *When the balance of the pool is right, the open water will be clear of algae and weed, and the plants and other inhabitants such as fish will look healthy and happy.*

creatures to move around freely. Another reason is that as soon as the pond becomes over-congested the plants will start to die through lack of nutrients, and the rotting vegetation will pollute the water.

Most water plants spread widely and quickly and, given the chance, they will cover the surface of the water; but they will also choke it below the surface. Once or twice a year some of the more rampant plants should be reduced. Oxygenators such as *Elodea canadensis* are the worst offenders. Fortunately, it is an easy job to clear an area of an invasive plant; just pull the plant out by the handful, leaving enough of it in place to produce oxygen and to restart the colonizing cycle.

THEN AND NOW

🍂 In the past, a garden pool was usually only a visual feature. Now it is often seen as a habitat that must be managed.

🍂 In earlier times, introducing plants and creatures suitable for creating a wildlife habitat was a matter of raiding a natural pond. Now natural stocks are diminishing and everything should be purchased from specialist centres.

VISUAL BALANCE

Another consideration is the visual balance. The amount of water lilies, for example, will affect the overall appearance of a pond. In most ponds the planting should not take up more than a third of the amount of open water, or the pond will seem crowded. On the margins some plants are more vigorous than others. At one extreme is *Typha latifolia*, reed mace, which will march through the shallow water throwing up its tall stems and obscuring all other plants. The balance can be controlled by pulling out any excess plants to reveal any hidden ones. This will also help to maintain the correct proportion of tall to low, and flowering to foliage, plants.

It is easy to keep the balance right if the gardener is completely in control, but unfortunately this is rarely the case. Vigilance must be kept at all times to ensure that vigorous plants that appear accidentally do not take root. For example, reed mace may not be introduced into small ponds but its seed is often blown in. Similarly, disease may appear in plants or animals. Problems should be dealt with quickly before they build up into a crisis.

ABOVE *Make sure the pool does not become overcrowded with plants – some can spread very rapidly. Remove excess plant material as necessary.*

PLANNING YOUR WATER GARDEN

*I*t is possible to start work, designing as you go, but much better to spend a bit of time drawing up a plan before you begin. Lists or notes about the overall effect you are hoping to achieve will help clarify the project and how you should go about it. Remember that there may be tasks, such as connecting up electrical devices, that you cannot do yourself, and this will affect the cost. Careful planning at the outset is rarely wasted.

You must consider the practicalities of site, size and shape when planning a water feature in your garden. The first is: where you are going to place it? This is both a practical and aesthetic question. A pool is best positioned where it will get maximum sunlight. Not only will the pool look more lively when it sparkles in the sun, but the plants and wildlife need the sun in order to thrive. Wind is also a factor – too much will break some of the taller plants, blow a fountain's spray beyond the pool and reduce water levels by creating excessive evaporation.

The size of a pond is mainly dictated by the size and layout of the garden; it should not be overbearing but sit comfortably in the overall design. There are other considerations. A large pond will take a lot of excavating and this may have to be done by hand if machinery cannot gain access. Similarly there is the problem of getting rid of vast

amounts of waste material. Another consideration might be the amount of planting you wish to include in the pond. The shape of your pond is an important consideration, as some shapes are more difficult to construct than others. Simplicity may be required in order to achieve good results. Access to water and electricity supplies might also be a consideration. There will be a lot of ground disruption and costs involved if you have to run these to a distant pond. Will the water necessary for filling and topping up the pond come from the mains, or can it be achieved by collecting surface water from roofs?

SITING THE POND

The pond must be sited in the best possible position. For example, if it is to be a long pond, then views down it from the house or another vantage point will be a great plus. The planting must be arranged in such away that it can be seen from the most visited areas. For example, if the pond is viewed from the house, the planting should be on the

LEFT *A water feature, no matter how small, should always be integrated into the overall* garden style. This formal pool fits in with the surrounding planting perfectly.

far side of the pond so that it can be seen reflected in the water. If the plants are on the near side the reflections are lost and the water obscured from sight. A sitting area next to a pond must not be screened from it by tall plants.

VISUAL QUALITIES AND PLANTING

The style and shape of the pond are both really important. For example, if the garden is a formal one then a formal water feature will be in keeping with this. An informal pond, on the other hand, is much more likely to fit in well with a 'casual' type of garden. Formal ponds are likely to be geometric with hard surrounds whereas informal types are more free-flowing. The planting in formal ponds is usually limited, with just a few well-chosen plants in key positions. The informal ones will have plants that reflect the more relaxed shape of the pond, and the proportion of open water to the planted area is likely to be much less.

The amount of planting you wish to establish around and in your water feature will also influence the design and position of it. If you want to grow a lot of plants in your pond, planting 'shelves' of different heights around the margins must be incorporated into the design. The pond must also be big enough to hold all the different types of plants you want to grow. If there is to be extensive planting beside the pond, there must be enough room to create either a border or a bog garden.

DRAWING UP THE PLAN

When you are ready to create your plan, write a list of all your requirements so that you have all the information in front of you. Draw out a rough sketch on paper to get some idea of what it will look like. Do not worry if you cannot draw, no one else will see it, but even the roughest of sketches will help you to foresee any difficulties. Once you have got the rough idea together, you can plot it out more accurately on squared paper, to scale. This is your final plan and it allows you to see if everything fits well before you start digging.

BELOW *Water can be brought right up to the house if desired, like this attractive stream that can be enjoyed from the patio or from the bridge.*

AN ORNAMENTAL POOL

*I*t is quite possible to have pools and ponds that contain no plants at all, their attraction relying on the shape of the pool or pond itself. Plants, however, enhance the appearance of a pool as well as providing it with a natural habitat for wildlife. Just as in other types of gardening, there are various styles of planting that can be adopted, according to personal preference or to blend in with the look of the rest of the garden. Planting may be formal and minimal, emphasizing the pond shape, or informal and naturalistic.

A formal pool usually has a regular shape such as a circle, square or rectangle and the planting is very restricted, often using just a hint of foliage. It is the open area of water that counts here, as this reinforces the shape of the pond and creates a simple clear-cut surface. In a rectangular pool there may be a basket of irises planted in each corner, or a small patch of water lilies in the centre. Informal pools will have much denser planting and a wider variety of plants both in and around the water.

PLANTING IN THE POOL

In an ornamental pool such as the one in the plan shown here the planting is quietly relaxed rather than rigidly formal. The pool depends more on a balance between shape, water and plants for its interest. The outline of the pool is still important, but it is less likely to be part of a grand design than a more formal pool, so it does not matter if the edges are obscured in places. The position of the

HINTS AND TOPS

❧ Do not overcrowd either the banks or the surface of the water with plants.
❧ Choose plants that have strong characteristics rather than background plants.
❧ Set the plants on ledges around the pool, depending on the depth of water each plant prefers to grow in.

plants in the pool is a matter of taste. There are a few common sense rules, however. The plants should be in distinct clumps so each can be seen and appreciated. Oxygenating plants, such as *Elodea*, can be grown in this type of pool, but they should be kept under strict control. Other plants can be planted in baskets and placed either on ledges or on the bottom of the pool, according to their required planting depth in the water.

AROUND THE EDGES

Most of the planting takes place in the pool. This is because the outline of the pool will be defined by them, and that most ornamental ponds have a liner; preventing the water entering the poolside bank, making most banks too dry for water plants. Ordinary border plants can look good by water, although these need strong characteristics — such as the bold foliage of gunnera. *Gunnera manicata* (giant rhubarb), is good along the edge of large ponds but needs moist soil. *Alchemilla mollis* is a very good plant for this type of situation, as are some of the grasses, such as *Miscanthus*.

LEFT *Irises look very attractive when planted beside a pool. They are upright-growing, giving height, and come in a variety of flower colours for visual diversity.*

Some grasses, *among them this* Miscanthus *sinensis* (eulalia) *associate well with water.*

Arum lilies Zantedeschia aethiopica *are an excellent choice for growing alongside the pool edge.*

Wooden decking *provides an informal poolside area for relaxing. It has a gentler appearance than concrete or paving slabs.*

You can use *irises to add a splash of bold colour to the pond surrounds. Mixed colours also look good.*

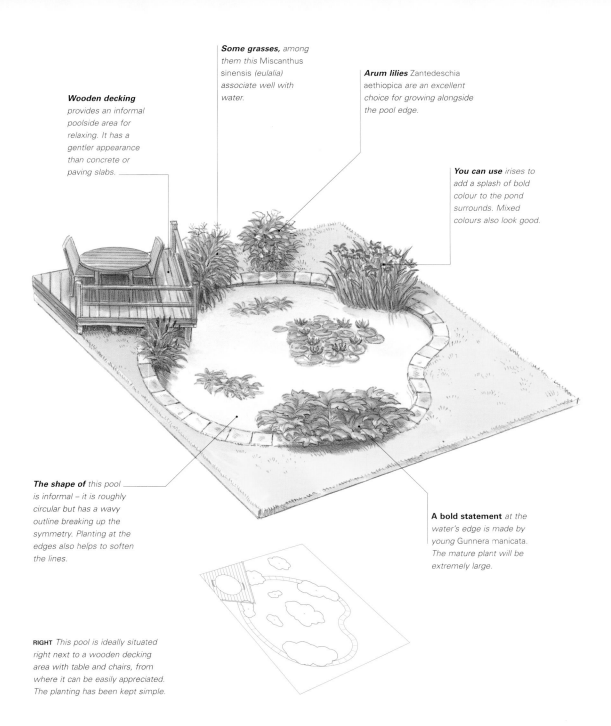

The shape of *this pool is informal – it is roughly circular but has a wavy outline breaking up the symmetry. Planting at the edges also helps to soften the lines.*

A bold statement *at the water's edge is made by young* Gunnera manicata. *The mature plant will be extremely large.*

RIGHT *This pool is ideally situated right next to a wooden decking area with table and chairs, from where it can be easily appreciated. The planting has been kept simple.*

23

A STREAMSIDE PLANTING

One of the most important aspects of water in the garden is movement. A stream provides this beautifully but, in the wild, streams usually support nothing more than a tangled mass of weedy vegetation on their banks. In a garden stream, more control of the plants is required, and therefore it is better to use ornamental plants than native ones, and to create the most naturalistic effect possible. There are many plants that are suitable for this purpose, depending on whether your stream is natural or artificial.

Very few people are lucky enough to have a natural stream running through their garden. Even those that do often find that it dries up during the summer months. The majority of water gardeners, therefore, have to make do with an artificial stream. If this is constructed and planted with care, however, it can be made to look natural. In reality, most natural streams have masses of untidy-looking plants in and around them, so a natural streamside planting in a garden should reflect that. The desired effect is that the plants should appear to be growing there naturally rather than having been planted there.

PLANTING THE STREAM

It is not too difficult to plant up a natural stream, since the water soaks into the banks, providing plenty of moisture for plants. In a garden setting, however, the majority of streams are artificial, which means that they are lined with a material such as concrete or a plastic liner. These, of course, retain the water as they are intended to do, and so

LEFT *Hostas are dramatic foliage plants that are ideal for planting beside a stream. Here* *the distinctive bright green ribbed leaves make a perfect foil for the grey slate.*

---

the banks are relatively dry. One way of coping with this is to make a broader stream, with areas of soil that are held in catchment areas along the bank. Alternatively, you can place stones in the flow of the water so that some of the water is splashed out to keep an adjacent area moist. Moisture-retentive soil also helps with this.

On the whole, most people prefer a natural-looking planting rather than placing plants according to a rigid plan. Generally this means planting in drifts; but, in a natural stream, pieces of plants are constantly breaking off, floating downstream and rooting to create individual plants dotted here and there. Why not try a random method of planting for a more authentic look?

For a natural stream planting, only native plants should be considered, and this can be very restrictive. A successful garden stream is likely to include plants such as some of the candelabra primulas, astilbes and hostas. If space allows, the large lysichitons should also be included. *Iris pseudacorus* (flag iris), *Lysimachia punctata* and a number of ferns could also be used.

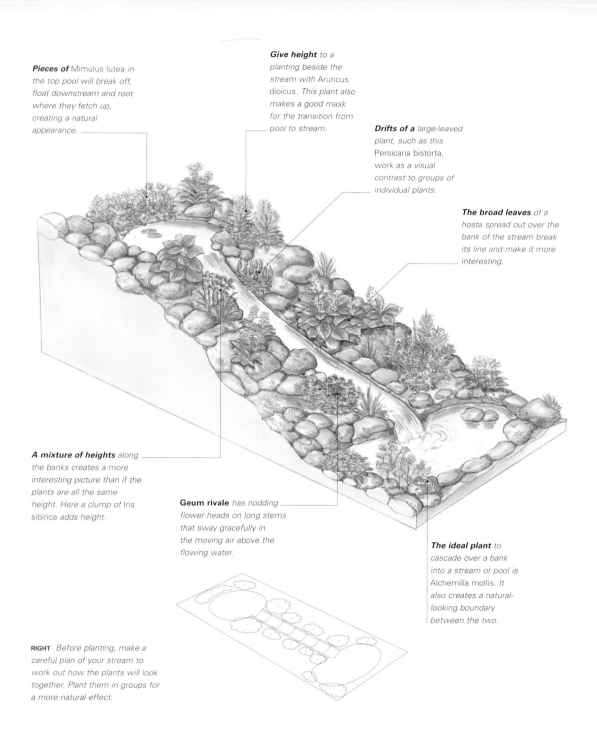

Pieces of Mimulus lutea *in the top pool will break off, float downstream and root where they fetch up, creating a natural appearance.*

Give height *to a planting beside the stream with* Aruncus dioicus. *This plant also makes a good mask for the transition from pool to stream.*

Drifts of a *large-leaved plant, such as this* Persicaria bistorta, *work as a visual contrast to groups of individual plants.*

The broad leaves *of a hosta spread out over the bank of the stream break its line and make it more interesting.*

A mixture of heights *along the banks creates a more interesting picture than if the plants are all the same height. Here a clump of* Iris sibirica *adds height.*

Geum rivale *has nodding flower heads on long stems that sway gracefully in the moving air above the flowing water.*

The ideal plant *to cascade over a bank into a stream or pool is* Alchemilla mollis. *It also creates a natural-looking boundary between the two.*

RIGHT *Before planting, make a careful plan of your stream to work out how the plants will look together. Plant them in groups for a more natural effect.*

25

A NATURAL POOL AND BOG GARDEN

The secret of creating a natural pool is to make it as authentic-looking as possible in both design (avoiding straight lines and covering any artificial liner) and planting. The area around a pond is usually dry, so in order to grow waterside plants it is necessary to create a bog garden, which is an area of ground that stays moist throughout the year. In essence, this is rather like creating a second pond with a liner, but instead of filling it with water, an organic-rich soil is used.

If possible a natural pool should be constructed in a natural way, using a clay base rather than an artificial liner. This is visually more attractive because there is no liner to disfigure the otherwise natural appearance. Plants can also be planted directly into the mud at the bottom of the pool, rather than being restricted to baskets as they would with a plastic liner. This allows them to spread in a more natural way. Grass banks are also more natural than ones lined with paving slabs, and it helps if one part of the bank has a gentle slope into the water, partly for appearance but also to allow animals to get to the water's edge.

The plants in and around the pool can normally be grown in water or boggy ground. For a really natural pool, use only native plants, but for a more interesting one exploit the complete range of ornamental garden plants. A natural pool usually has plenty of reeds and other vertical plants around the margins and even in some of the deeper water. This type of plant is desirable because its shape allows for part of it to be above water at all times.

Reeds can be invasive, however, so it may be better to achieve the same effect by using irises.

In the water itself, you can grow aquatic plants. The best known of these are water lilies. Such floating plants should be allowed to spread, but it is important, both for the life of the pond and for the visual effect, that they are not allowed to cover the whole surface of the pond.

THE BOG GARDEN

The bog garden is a natural extension of the pond and gives the water gardener the opportunity to grow a wider range of plants. In a natural pond, a bog might be a silted up area. In a garden, a bog must be created. Generally it is formed from a large hole lined with a flexible liner that is filled with a organic-rich soil. When the pond is full, it overflows into the area, keeping the soil moist. A large number of colourful plants can be grown here, planted in the same way as in a normal ornamental border.

LEFT *Although these steps made from sawn-off logs do not look very natural, the pond itself and its planting both give the appearance of having been left to their own devices.*

Trees are valuable in the design as they add height as well as shade to the scheme. Here Betula nigra fulfills the function.

Astilbes add splashes of frothy colour to a bog garden which can sometimes become overwhelmed with the greenness of the foliage.

The large, floating leaves of the lilies create areas of shade in the water which offer protection to water creatures.

Stepping stones allow access to the middle of the bog garden without the necessity of creating a proper path.

Grasses create fountains of narrow leaves which contrast well with the other types of foliage in the border.

Stands of vertical plants, such as this Iris laevigata, rise from the water create a tranquil image.

Yellow is a common colour amongst water plants and mixes well with all the greens and the reflective surface of the water.

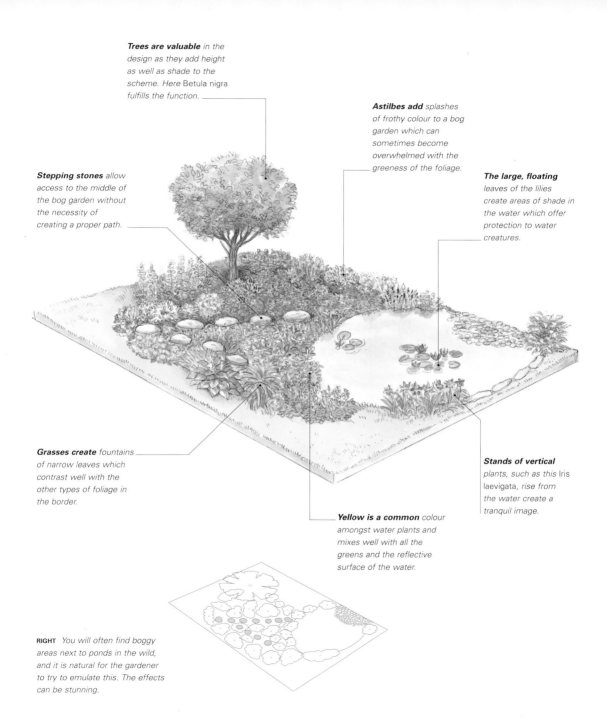

RIGHT You will often find boggy areas next to ponds in the wild, and it is natural for the gardener to try to emulate this. The effects can be stunning.

CREATING A WATER GARDEN

2

There is nothing more satisfying than relaxing beside a water garden or feature that you have created yourself. It pays to look at as many water features as you can, either in reality or in books and magazines, to collect ideas so that you can create something truly individual. This section covers all the practicalities of creating a water garden, as well as related aspects ranging from choosing fish to planting and propagation. It also includes several interesting projects that can be adapted to fit your own garden scheme.

LEFT *Once the initial effort of constructing your water garden is finished, you will be able to sit back and enjoy the fruits of your labour.*

EDGING THE POND · CHOICES

PAVING

Paving is one of the easiest ways of creating an edge to a pond. It not only forms a firm base on which to stand but also prevents any erosion of the banks. Another big advantage of using paving slabs as edging is that they can be used to disguise the liners as they emerge from the pond. This can be done by making sure the slabs project a little way out over the water.

It is vital that any slabs used on the edge of the pond are well bedded and secure. Any movement of the slabs may result in somebody falling into the water. Always use non-slip slabs.

Natural-coloured slabs usually look better than brightly coloured ones, and paving slabs work well with more formal pools.

CHOICE PLANTS CHECKLIST

- *Alisma plantago-aquatica* (water plantain)
- *Caltha palustris* (marsh marigold)
- *Cotula coronopifolia* (brass buttons)
- *Iris laevigata* (Japanese water iris)
- *Mentha aquatica* (water mint)
- *Mimulus luteus* (monkey musk)

DECKING

Wooden decking is one of the most versatile forms of edging as it is not limited to the shape of the pool. It can follow the edge or it can jut out over the water, even to the extent of bridging the pond at a narrow point. A deck jutting out over the water makes an ideal place to sit and relax, and it can be given additional decoration by placing containers of plants next to the seating area.

It is easier to use the wood in straight lines, but the decking can be shaped to follow the contours of the pond. Hardwood is the best timber to use for decking and the fixings should be galvanized to prevent rusting. If you do use softwood instead, make sure you treat it with a preservative that is non-toxic to both plants and wildlife.

CHOICE PLANTS CHECKLIST

- *Acorus calamus* (sweet flag)
- *Alisma plantago-aquatica* (water plantain)
- *Pontederia cordata* (pickerel weed)
- *Schoenoplectus lacustris* subsp. *tabernaemontani* 'Zebrinus'
- *Typha latifolia* (bulrush)
- *Zantedeschia aethiopica* (arum lily)

PEBBLE EDGING

Large pebbles provide an ideal informal edging and are useful when you want to create a natural look. They can be laid in a drift to form a sloping bank down into the pond. Gravel can also be used, but the smaller stones can get knocked into the pond. If you use gravel as part of a mixed surface, however, alongside paving slabs or granite setts, it works much more satisfactorily.

It is best to use a mixture of pebble sizes as this looks more natural. They should also be tipped into the pond so that the 'beach' runs from on top of the bank to below the surface of the water. Choose pebbles that will blend in with the surroundings. Small plants placed in and among the pebbles will enhance the natural appearance.

CHOICE PLANTS CHECKLIST

- *Carex riparia* (greater pond sedge)
- *Houttuynia cordata*
- *Juncus effusus* 'Spiralis' (corkscrew rush)
- *Narthecium ossifragum* (bog asphodel)
- *Ranunculus lingua* (greater spearwort)
- *Veronica beccabunga* (brooklime)

GRASS/PLANTED EDGE

One of the simplest-looking edges is a lawn that runs straight up to the rim of the pond; but in some ways this is the least attractive, as the lawn cannot jut out over the edge to hide the liner.

Using plants to form a border is much more satisfactory as they will hang over the edge, disguising the liner. They will also create a colourful display that will be reflected on the surface of the water. *Alchemilla mollis* (lady's mantle) is one of the best plants for trailing over and disguising the edge of ponds. Plants set beyond the edge of the liner should be ordinary garden plants, since bog and other moisture-loving plants will find it too dry. A special bog garden can also be created (*see pages 54–5*) to give an even more natural look.

CHOICE PLANTS CHECKLIST

- *Alchemilla mollis* (lady's mantle)
- *Butomus umbellatus* (flowering rush)
- *Eriophorum angustifolium* (cotton grass)
- *Iris pseudacorus* (yellow flag)
- *Myosotis scorpioides* (water forget-me-not)
- *Sagittaria sagittifolia* (arrow head)

VARIETY IN FOUNTAINS • CHOICES

JETS

A wide range of jets is available. They vary from those that produce a single narrow stream to ones that produce a variety of shapes, such as tiered sprays. All these jets are produced in a similar fashion; only the shape of the nozzle alters the pattern. The shape of the jet also influences the sound; those with finer sprays make a softer sound than those with large drops. Some spray patterns look spectacular when lit up at night, and the surrounding plants will also be lit up.

The height and size of the jet should be in keeping with the pool and the effect of the wind taken into account. A tall jet with a fine spray will be blown a great distance from its starting point, which means that it is likely to fall outside the pool.

CHOICE PLANTS CHECKLIST

- Leave clear water around jets as few plants will be tolerant of water constantly beating down on them.
- *Aponogeton distachyos* (water hawthorn)
- *Nuphar lutea* (brandy bottle)

DECORATIVE FOUNTAINS

Sculptural fountains can make excellent central features in a garden. They can take the form of a classical urn-type shape or something with a figurative design. The urn-type fountain can consist of a single bowl or a series of bowls of decreasing size. They work well with a simple jet or several finer ones creating a simple pattern. Figurative designs can involve animals, people or even plants. With these designs, it is important that the shape and direction of the spray is relevant to the design. Modern abstract designs that are made from a variety of materials, including steel and glass, can also be used. Classical fountains usually look best in formal situations, but modern ones can be used in a whole variety of positions.

CHOICE PLANTS CHECKLIST

- Round-leafed floating plants placed near the fountain will complement the ripples in the water.
- *Aponogeton distachyos* (water hawthorn)
- *Nuphar lutea* (brandy bottle)
- *Nymphaea* (water lilies)

WALL SPOUTS

Fountains do not need to be set in the middle of a pool. A popular alternative, especially suitable for small gardens, is a wall spout. This consists of a pipe set in a wall emitting single or multiple trickles of water. They can, of course, be jets of water that fall into a pool or a disguised reservoir covered in pebbles. The pipe usually comes out of the wall through the mouth of a face mask, often that of a lion. Alternatively, a spout can be used to give the appearance that the water comes from a spring or old pump. You can buy reproductions of old hand-pumps that constantly circulate water so that it trickles into a trough or barrel. A water spout can be fixed to a specially built brick column if there is no suitable wall available.

CHOICE PLANTS CHECKLIST

- Plant mainly foliage plants around the outside of the container into which the water falls, to create a slightly derelict, Gothic look.
- *Astilbe* x *arendsii* (astilbe)
- *Athyrium filix-femina* (lady fern)
- *Hosta crispula*
- *Iris ensata* (Japanese iris)
- *Juncus effusus* 'Spiralis' (corkscrew rush)

BUBBLE JETS

While most traditional fountains consist of a jet or spout of water, modern fountains are often little more than an eruption of water that simply bubbles out of the ground or through a stone. The best example of this is an old mill stone. The water bubbles up through the centre of the stone, trickles to the edge and then disappears into the pebbles that surround it. Beneath the stone is a hidden reservoir that collects the water and houses the pump. This produces a very gentle, low-key fountain that is suitable for small gardens. It is especially useful in gardens where there are young children, as there are no pools of standing water. Plant around the outside of the feature, but be careful not to obscure it with tall plants.

CHOICE PLANTS CHECKLIST

- *Geum rivale* (water avens)
- *Hosta* 'Frances Williams'
- *Houttuynia cordata* 'Chameleon'
- *Juncus effusus* 'Spiralis' (corkscrew rush)
- *Mentha aquatica* (water mint)
- *Mimulus cardinalis* (scarlet monkey flower)
- *Phalaris arundinacea* var. *picta* (ribbon grass)

FISH • CHOICES

GOLDFISH

Goldfish are one of the easiest types of fish to obtain and look after. They will tolerate a wide range of conditions and are hardy. Goldfish create a wonderfully lively picture in a pool, so it is often nice to create a seating area beside it to watch them from. They are usually orange-red in colour, although they can vary from cream through to red with touches of black. They do not attain their full colour until their second year and may lose it again in old age. The average length is about 15cm (6in) but in favourable conditions they can grow up to 25cm (10in) or even bigger. If there is plenty of space they will breed freely, but in more restricted areas the adults are likely to eat all the young fry before they have had a chance to mature.

CHOICE CHECKLIST

❧ There are fancy varieties of goldfish, such as the veiltails with long fins. These are less hardy than ordinary goldfish.

❧ Goldfish soon learn to come to be fed if you want to feed them by hand.
❧ The more fancy types of goldfish will need protection over the winter months.

KOI

Koi have a particularly wonderful range of colours and markings and they can grow to very large sizes – up to 45cm (18in) or more. They can be destructive, however, and will soon empty a small pond of all plants. For this reason they are not good fish to have in a natural-looking pond. A large pond will be able to accommodate one or two without too much of a problem.

If you want to collect koi, then build ponds specially for them; they should be among filtration plants and have constantly recirculating water. Specimen fish can be very expensive, and as they need their own particular conditions they are really better for fish enthusiasts than for people who just want a few fish to add to their garden pond.

CHOICE CHECKLIST

❧ Koi quickly learn to be fed by hand.
❧ Koi can live for up to a hundred years and individual fish are usually seen as special pets by their owners.

❧ There should be a distinct boundary placed between the different colours of the more special specimens in order to prevent the colours being mixed.

3

GOLDEN ORFE

Golden orfe are long slender-bodied fish, with a snub nose that makes them look almost tubular. They can reach up to 45cm (18in) and will grow particularly fast in their first few years. They are golden-orange in colour and, unlike many other fish, show this colour almost straight after emerging from their eggs. Their undersides are silver and they frequently have small black markings on their backs. Golden orfe make especially attractive fish for a pond because they are surface-feeders and can be easily observed as they shoot from the water to capture gnats, mosquitoes and other insects. They will also often leap in the spray of fountains and falling water. They will occasionally breed in an outside pool, but it needs to be a large one.

CHOICE CHECKLIST

∾ These fish will quickly become tame if hand-fed.
∾ The golden orfe is a good choice of fish for a larger pond, especially if there is also a fountain.

∾ The common orfe is similar to the golden orfe except that (as is implied by its other name, silver orfe) it is silver all over.

4

RUDD

Not all pond-owners necessarily want colourful or exotic fish. Those with natural ponds will probably prefer a native fish that seems more in keeping with the nature of the pond. The rudd may be a very good choice for this. It has a silver body and bright red fins that glow in the water. Rudds like a large pond with plenty of plants in it and areas of open water where they can enjoy the sun. They multiply quite quickly if conditions are right and fish of all sizes can be seen swimming together in large shoals. The largest fish are usually about 20cm (8in) long, but they will sometimes grow bigger than this. They also eat filamentous algae and thus help to keep the pond clear. In winter and cooler periods they will disappear among the pond weeds.

CHOICE CHECKLIST

∾ This is an ideal fish for a natural pond that has plenty of vegetation and other wildlife in it.
∾ It is not as vividly coloured as many exotic fish.

∾ In larger ponds these fish do not require feeding.
∾ Rudd will eat algae and therefore help to keep the water clear.

BUYING AND PROPAGATING WATER PLANTS

P*lants that are to be grown in the pool margins, on the banks and in bog gardens are easy to buy, plant and propagate, just like ordinary garden plants. For those that are either submerged or float in the water, however, a little more thought and care will be needed. Such plants have to be kept in water at all times — but this is not difficult to achieve once you know how, and you will soon feel confident enough to start propagating them as well.*

Some general nurseries and garden centres carry a few water plants, but it is better to go to specialist nurseries to purchase them. They not only stock a wider range of material but are also equipped to keep plants in tanks, in the best possible conditions. Never buy dried-out specimens. When buying submerged or floating plants, bear in mind that they can be left out of water long enough to get them home, but then they should be planted straight away. Never leave them in the hot sun. If you cannot plant them immediately, put them in a bucket of water.

PROPAGATION

Bog-garden plants, as well as those that grow on the bank or in very shallow water, can be propagated in the same way as ordinary garden plants. However, they should be given a moisture-retentive compost and should also be watered frequently to make sure that they stay moist. The easiest and most often used method of propagation is division. Almost all of the water and marginal plants can be divided. The best time to do this is in spring, just as the water temperature is beginning to rise and the plants are coming into growth. It is also easy to grow many of these plants from seed. Bog plants and shallow-water plants are sown in the same way as any other plant, but remember that plants that live mainly below water need to be kept in water at all times.

Most submerged plants are propagated from cuttings. This really is a very easy process: just cut a few healthy stems and place them in a lattice pot filled with compost. Then cover the compost with a layer of gravel and submerge the pot in water (this can be in the pond itself or in a bucket of water). The stems will quickly root and spread through the pond. Plants that creep across the mud on the edge and in the shallow water can also be increased from cuttings. In these cases the pot should be placed in a shallow

ABOVE *Water plants should be purchased from specialist nurseries in the first instance, but then it can be fun to try creating your own new plants through propagation.*

container of water but not entirely submerged. Stems that already bear roots can be cut from many of these plants. These can just be potted up or planted directly into the margin of the pond.

Water lilies can be increased from seed, but an easier method is to use 'eyes'. These appear on the rootstock of the lilies and look like miniature plants with juvenile foliage. Plants should be removed from the pond in spring or early summer, and then you can cut as many eyes from them as you need. Then powder the cuts with sulphur and return the plants to the pool. Place the eyes in individual pots of compost and stand them in water so that the rims of the pots are just covered. Grow on until the plants are large enough to plant out.

SOWING SEED OF WATER PLANTS

1 Fill a 9cm (3½in) pot with a seed compost. Lightly firm it down and level the surface.

2 Sow the seed thinly on the top of the compost. Spread it so that it is evenly spaced across the surface.

3 Cover the seed and compost with a layer of fine gravel. The gravel will prevent the lighter parts of the compost and the seeds floating away.

4 Place the pot in a container and pour in water until it is just below the level of the compost. (If you are sowing water lily seeds then fill it to just above the top of the gravel.) Leave in water until germinated.

5 Prick out the seedlings into individual pots, using a special water-garden compost. Cover the top with gravel and re-immerse the plants in water.

HINTS AND TIPS

🍃 Use a pole with a hook on the end when removing lattice pots from a large water feature.

🍃 Always keep pots of submerged plants in a tank or other container of water.

🍃 Do not leave pots full of bog plants standing in water, but make certain that the plants are watered regularly to keep the compost moist.

TECHNIQUE **DIVIDING MARGINAL PLANTS**

1 Lift the lattice pots from the water and take the plant out. Cut off any roots that are sticking through the side of the pot and are preventing the plant from being removed.

2 Under a tap or in a bucket of water, wash off all the soil from the roots.

3 Gently pull the plant into separate pieces. Some plants will easily fall apart, while others may need to be cut with a knife. Make certain that each of the divisions includes a growing point or bud.

4 Pot each division into individual pots, repotting any large pieces directly into a lattice pot to be returned immediately to the water.

PLANTING WATER PLANTS

*T*he technique for planting water plants is slightly different from conventional planting because they are usually planted into a lined pond that has no soil of its own. It is also obviously quite difficult to reach into the middle of a pond. Simple methods have been devised, however, to overcome these problems, mainly involving the use of 'lattice' pots lined with hessian. Planting in a bog garden is more conventional because soil is involved.

The key to planting in water is to use lattice pots or baskets (*see opposite*). These are widely available from nurseries and water-garden centres and come in a variety of sizes. The advantage is that they allow water and gases to pass freely through the sides. However, they also allow compost to flow out in the opposite direction. To prevent this, pots should be lined with hessian before they are filled with a special aquatic planting compost. General potting compost is not suitable as it is very fibrous and light, so much of it will float away. To help retain the compost you use, as well as to anchor the plant in the pot, cover the top with a layer of gravel or small stones. This will also prevent any fish from disturbing the compost.

> ### HINTS AND TIPS
>
> ❧ Do not use conventional plastic flower pots for plants that grow in water.
> ❧ Use a special aquatic planting compost.
> ❧ Plant in spring or early summer, just as the plants are coming into growth.
> ❧ When planting, ensure that there are no strands of algae on the new plants.
> ❧ Always top compost with gravel to stop the plant and lighter components of the compost from floating away.
> ❧ Different plants require different planting depths. This is achieved by using ledges of varying heights.

Marginal plants that are placed around the pond require different depths of water and are stood on ledges of different heights around the edge. Deep-water plants, such as water lilies and oxygenators, are planted at the bottom of the pond. Bog plants are planted into the soil at the side of the pond. This soil should be moist but not waterlogged. It is possible to reach out and put pots with marginal plants onto their ledges, but is more difficult to place plants further out. However, with the use of strong string and two people it is achievable (*see opposite*).

The best time for planting is spring or early summer. When water lilies are planted, they will often float to the surface, coming out of their pots. To prevent this, remove their leaves, as they can grow another set once they are firmly rooted. Alternatively, leave potted plants in a bucket of water for a couple of weeks so that they grow into their compost before being put into deep water.

LEFT *If planted correctly, your water and marginal plants should eventually grow lush foliage and flower profusely. Most will need a special aquatic compost in order to thrive.*

TECHNIQUE   LOWERING POTS INTO DEEPER WATER

1 Thread two long strings, each longer than the diameter of the pond, through the sides of the lattice pot you want to place in the water.

2 You will now need a helper. Each person takes one end of both of the strings and lifts so that the basket is suspended between you.

3 Move to opposite sides of the pond, so that the basket is suspended between the two of you, and is now suspended over the water.

4 Move the basket to the required position, then gently lower it into the water. Once it is in the pond, one person releases the strings and the other carefully pulls them out of the lattice pot without disturbing its position.

TECHNIQUE   USING A LATTICE POT

1 Line the lattice pot with hessian sacking so that the compost does not float out through the sides of the pot.

2 Fill the pot with a special aquatic planting compost. Water the compost so that it is thoroughly soaked.

3 Top up with more compost, as it sinks when watered, and then repeat the process of watering.

4 Place your chosen plant into the prepared compost and firm it in gently.

5 Cover the compost with 1cm (½in) of gravel or small stones to help keep the lighter bits of the compost from floating away, and to keep the plant in place.

6 Finally, place the planted-up lattice pot in the water at the appropriate depth. Make certain that the pot is sitting firmly in position so that it does not topple over.

AFTERCARE AND MAINTENANCE

*O*nce *a water feature has been built, and the plants and wildlife introduced, most of the work has been done, but you cannot now abandon it. A certain amount of care and attention is required to keep it looking its best. Fortunately, the work is neither difficult nor particularly time-consuming, and consists of removing weeds and dead material regularly, feeding plants, cleaning out the pond if necessary, and a number of other seasonal tasks.*

The main task when looking after a pond or pool is to keep it tidy. Remove any dead vegetation as it appears during spring and summer, and take out any plants that die as soon as you can. The main clear-up occurs in late winter when all the dead vegetation from the previous year should be removed. You should also cut back old stems and leaves to the base of plants both in the pond and in the bog garden.

The bog garden should also be weeded and the surface of the soil lightly forked over. It is a good idea to mulch the surface to help keep the weeds down and to hold the moisture in the soil. Do not use organic materials such as farmyard manure, however, as these are too rich in nutrients; if they reach the pond they will encourage algae to form. Instead use chipped bark or leaf mould.

Basic 'weeding' in a pond consists of removing any algae that may have formed a blanket over the surface of the water. It is best to do this manually using a rake. You can suspend a bale of

RIGHT *Keep areas of water clear of algae and other plants, to maintain the balance of the pool.*

| TECHNIQUE | USING STRAW TO STOP ALGAE FORMING |

1 Remove all the algae you can from the pond using a rake or stick. Place a bale of barley straw inside a hessian sack, which will prevent bits of the straw floating up to the surface.

2 Add some bricks or rocks to the hessian sack. This will help the bale to sink to the bottom of the pond when you place it in the water.

3 Water the sack thoroughly to remove the air from the bale, or it will float. Place it in the water and let it sink. It can now be left in place until autumn. A new bale should be put in during spring.

1 Use a lawn rake to remove filamentous algae. Turn the rake upside down and push it into the water below the algae.

2 Lift the rake once it holds as much algae as you can lift. Remove it from the pond area and clear the rake of algae before putting it back in the water.

3 A rake can also be used to sweep across the water at an angle to remove any loose algae from the surface.

4 When clearing algae from among plants, use a long cane with a hook in the end. Insert this and twist it round so the algae wind onto the stick.

POINTS TO CONSIDER

• Do not let a concrete pool freeze over completely in winter as it will starve fish and plants of oxygen, eventually killing them.
• Prevent leaves and other dead or dying vegetation from rotting in the pond by removing them quickly.
• Remove all algae on sight, do not let it build up.
• Avoid using an algicide if at all possible as it has too many hazardous qualities.

in the water in a hessian sack to help to prevent algae from forming (*see opposite*). As a last resort, you could use an algicide, but this may also kill off other plants so is better avoided. If you do use an algicide, always remove the dead algae as this can pollute the water. The other type of weeding that is needed from time to time is to cut back any plant that has grown too big. Oxygenators can grow at a rapid pace and will soon fill the pool. They need to be cut back to ensure there is plenty of open water, otherwise they may do more harm than good.

If the water has turned black it will be necessary to clean the pond out completely. This is best done in early spring and involves draining the pool by syphoning the water out. Catch any fish, and as much of the natural wildlife as you can, and keep them in containers in a cool

place. Wash out the pool, clean off the plants and return the fish and wildlife to the pool once it has been refilled and the temperature has returned to normal.

The other thing that you must do in spring is feed the plants in the pond. This is done by pushing a fertilizer ball or sachet into the compost in every basket next to each plant. There is no need to feed recently repotted plants.

SEASONAL CARE

In summer, and at other times when there are drying winds, it is essential to keep an eye on the water level of the pool and to top it up if necessary. In autumn you should cover the pond with a net to keep out the leaves. In winter the main hazard is frost. Most pools with flexible liners are not troubled by the expansion caused by frost, but it can crack a concrete pool. To combat this, float a rubber ball or piece of polystyrene in the water to absorb the expansion. Also drain any pipes that lie above the level of the soil or just below the surface since they might freeze over in cold weather.

It is also vital to keep part of the pond's surface ice-free in winter because noxious gases can collect under the frozen surface and kill both plants and fish. You can install a special water heater. If your pond does freeze over, never use a hammer to break the ice. Instead, hold a saucepan of hot water on the surface until it melts a hole.

CONSTRUCTING A POND

*I*t is not as difficult as you may think to construct your own pond. One of the most important considerations is the material to be used for the base. Although concrete has its advantages for formal ponds, it is difficult to install. Pond liners are a simple alternative and with care will be trouble-free. They are also quick: a small pool can be created in a weekend. There are two common types of liner available — flexible liners made of black butyl rubber, and preformed rigid liners made of fibreglass or plastic.

Before you start digging, one of the first things to check is that the banks of the pond will be level. A pond that is half-empty at one end and full at the other looks most peculiar. So, after working out the shape you want your pond to be, the next thing is to put in some pegs, which will be your level guides (*see below*).

For a small pool, and for those who have limited access to their back gardens, hand-digging is the only option. Mechanical diggers speed up the operation considerably but unless you do it yourself it is not easy to have precise control on what is dug out and where it is dumped, also, they can be expensive. It is essential that you determine

TECHNIQUE	INSTALLING A FLEXIBLE POND LINER

1 Mark out the shape of the pond. For irregular shapes use a flexible hosepipe. Knock in pegs around the outline of the pond and check their tops with a spirit-level. It is essential that they all come up to the same level, so double-check them.

2 Dig a shallow trench, about 15cm (6in) deep around the site, measuring down from the tops of the pegs to ensure that it is horizontal. This will be where the liner finishes and where the surface of the water will eventually be.

3 About 30cm (12in) further in, dig a second, deeper, trench about 30cm (12in) around the whole pond. Dig out all the soil across the site so that a shallow pond is created.

4 About another 30cm (12in) further in, dig another trench about 45cm (18in) deep. Once again, dig out the remaining soil across the pond to form its base. Line the whole of the pond with a special liner underlay, or cover it with a thick layer of old newspapers or sand.

5 Lay the liner across the pond and hold it in place with bricks or stones. Slowly fill the pond with water so that the liner gradually sinks into position.

6 When the pond is full of water, trim off the excess liner, leaving enough to cover the first shallow ledge. Cover the edges either with soil or with paving slabs. You can now plant around it to soften the edges if you wish.

- Do not buy a cheap liner, as unseen stones might easily penetrate it and become a real nuisance.
- Use the best liner you can afford and avoid polythene.
- Bury the ends of the liner vertically about 30cm (12in) beyond the rim of the pond.
- Avoid cavities under a rigid liner. Push sand down the sides until all gaps are filled and the pool is stable.

where you are putting the soil before you start. Allow plenty of space and keep the topsoil separate from the subsoil as this can be used elsewhere.

The pond may just be a simple hole, but if you are intending to plant it up then remember to create some ledges of varying depths. This will allow you to grow deep-water plants as well as marginal ones. Digging should be done one level at a time, until you have the completed shape of the pond. If desired, a shallowly sloping bank that allows a 'beach' for smaller plants can also be added.

USING FLEXIBLE LINERS
You will need to fill the dug hole with a soft material such as special underlay to prevent any stones from piercing the liner. Alternatively, sand can be used on the horizontal surfaces, and layers of newspapers on the vertical ones. Then stretch the liner right across the pond and weight down the

edges with bricks and stones so that it is taut. Fill the centre of the liner with water, and as it fills it will sink into the hole, dragging the bricks across the surrounding surface. This method will keep the liner wrinkle-free.

When the pond is full, trim the liner, leaving plenty of overlap. This should be buried in the bank a little way below ground level. It can be hidden under paving slabs, but often the best way of disguising it is by planting irises, for example, around the margins of the pool or by having plants such as *Alchemilla mollis* hanging over the edge.

USING RIGID LINERS
Preformed pools are becoming available in a wider range of shapes and can be easier to install. The shapes usually include built-in planting ledges that lattice pots can stand on. The hole should be dug and lined in the same way as for a flexible liner – just remember to ensure that the hole you dig is the same shape as the preformed pool! It is also essential to check that the pool is level, or parts of the plastic will show above the waterline. After inserting the pool, fill in any cavities around it with sand.

EXTRA EQUIPMENT
Little extra equipment is needed. If algae disfigure the pond a filtration plant may help. There is a variety of types, which will be stocked at any good nursery specializing in water gardens. A bale of barley straw may be a cheap alternative.

TECHNIQUE — **INSTALLING A RIGID POND LINER**

1 Stand the pool level on the site and mark around the edges with canes or pegs. Dig out the soil within the marks down to the level of the first ledge.

2 Then place the pool in the resulting hole and similarly mark around the base. Dig out the soil from within this mark to the full depth of the pool. The resulting hole should be slightly bigger than the liner.

3 Line the hole with sand and insert the liner. Check that the pool is level in all directions and then ram more sand down the sides to make certain that it is stable.

WATERFALLS AND CASCADES

Features with falling water are not as easy to construct as a pond. The benefits that the moving water bring to the garden, however, make the effort more than worthwhile. Unless you are lucky enough to have natural water emerging at the top of a slope, in the form of a stream or spring, you will need to install a pump. This will mean providing a supply of electricity to the garden, so it is wise to plan carefully before you start.

Waterfalls and cascades (a series of waterfalls) may be situated within streams, or join one pool to another. In a stream, a waterfall can be created by placing a row of stones across its bed. With two pools, just lower the rim in one place of the upper pool so that the water runs over the edge into the lower one. Waterfalls and associated streams can be constructed using flexible liners or rigid preformed sections that are readily available. In a small garden, you can have water tumbling down a vertical wall into a narrow pool by using a hidden reservoir.

The construction of a cascade is similar to that of a single waterfall, except that you are obviously creating a series of falls rather than just one. It will need a greater slope in the land. A natural stream can be dammed with low walls across it at intervals, or widened in places into a series of pools, each dropping into the other. An artificial stream can be built on a slope to resemble a natural stream, using rocks, or you can make it look, for example, like a brick stairway with water tumbling down it.

PUMPS

You will need a pump to recycle the water from the bottom to the top. The size of pump will depend on the volume of water – a fast, wide waterfall will need a more powerful pump than will a trickle. Professional assistance in choosing the right one will be provided at the better water centres. Pumps need electricity and if you have any doubts about installing it safely, get a qualified electrician to do it.

TECHNIQUE   **MEASURING THE WATER FLOW**

1 To determine the size of pump you will need for running a stream or waterfall, first measure the width of the stream or fall.

2 Make up a plank with two pieces of wood nailed to it, at the same width as the stream or waterfall.

3 Place a hosepipe on the plank. Adjust the flow from the pipe until it produces the same rate of flow between the side pieces that you will require of the finished stream.

4 When satisfied, place a bucket underneath and catch the water for exactly one minute. Measure the volume, and this will supply the flow rate needed to select the pump.

PROJECT | **MAKING A WATERFALL**

1 Draw up a plan and use it to mark out the design. Create the main pool (*see pages 42–3*) so that it comes right up to the bank over which the waterfall will be. At the top of the bank, dig another pool.

2 Between the two, build a brick wall on a shallow concrete foundation. The top of the wall must be the same level as the water in the top pool, but the chute from which water will pour should be a brick lower.

- *Adiantum venustum*
- *Alchemilla mollis* (lady's mantle)
- *Athyrium filix-femina* (lady fern)
- *Blechnum spicant* (hard fern)
- *Cardamine pratensis* (cuckoo flower)
- *Geum rivale* (water avens)
- *Hosta crispula*
- *Iris laevigata* (Japanese water iris)
- *Mimulus luteus* (monkey musk)
- *Salix hastata* 'Wehrhahnii'

3 Making sure to use an underlay, line the bottom pool, first bringing the liner up over the wall. Then line the top pool, leaving a generous overlap to hang down over the wall into the lower pool.

4 Place underlay on the chute and cement in a 5cm (2in) thick slab of stone or concrete so that it overhangs the lower pool slightly. Cover the top of the wall and the exposed liner with irregular stones.

5 Place a pump in the lower pool, then disguise the exit pipe with stones or plants and run it through a trench to the upper pool into which the water should enter from beneath a rock.

PLANTING WATERFALLS AND CASCADES

Foliage plants look really good beside a waterfall. Ferns grow naturally by water and are therefore ideal. The fine-cut fronds of *Adiantum venustum* are good as they froth out in imitation of the falling water. Hostas also work well, especially among rocks, as do vertical plants. In a rocky situation, a craggy willow such as *Salix hastata* 'Wehrhahnii' would be in keeping as long as it is not allowed to get too large. Position these plants on one side of the waterfall rather than directly under it. They can be planted in the soil or placed in pots hidden among the rocks.

RIGHT *This waterfall has been cleverly designed with rocks, logs and plants to look very natural. Ferns are ideal beside a waterfall as they thrive in a humid atmosphere.*

DEEP-WATER PLANTS

For most people, a water plant lives completely in the water, either growing below the surface or floating on it. These deep-water plants have adapted to fill a particular niche, and are relatively free from competition from the greater number of plants that will grow in a lesser depth of water round the margins. They are not necessarily the most glamorous of plants, but they have a distinct role to play in the overall appearance of the pond, as well as in maintaining its physical wellbeing.

Submerged plants are the ones that immediately come to the minds of most people when they think about deep-water plantings. These below-surface plants are not the most beautiful in the plant kingdom. They are practical (because they produce oxygen and remove excess nutrients) rather than ornamental. Having said that, some, such as *Myriophyllum aquaticum* (parrot's feather), are attractive when they poke up above the water level; but once they are taken out of the water they collapse and become an unattractive sodden mass. Because of their underwater position they have insignificant flowers, so the main attraction is their foliage.

Most submerged plants are geared to reproduce by either spreading and rooting as they go, or through pieces breaking off and rooting where they land. This means that most spread very quickly, and in smaller ponds it may be necessary to pull out the excess several times a year to prevent the water from becoming choked.

These plants are easily increased. For most, you can tie a few stems into a bundle with a piece of wire (rather than string, as the wire acts as a weight) and then drop it into the mud or silt at the bottom of the pool to root. In a clean pool, the stems can be inserted into a pot of compost and then lowered into the water.

DEEP WATER AQUATICS

Floating water plants that are anchored include plants such as *Nymphaea* (water lilies) and *Nuphar* (brandy bottles). These plants are far more decorative. They not only generally have very beautiful flowers in a wide range of colours but their foliage, which floats flat on the surface, is also attractive. They root on the bottom and have long stems attached to the leaves. When planting these types of plant, it is important to start them off in shallow water and gradually move them into deeper water as the stems lengthen. Most tend to spread quite rapidly and must be kept under

TECHNIQUE	INCREASING SUBMERGED PLANTS

1 Take two or three stems of the plant, each about 15cm (6in) long, and twist a piece of wire or a strip of lead around them to make a neat bundle.

2 Drop the bundle into the pond so that it sinks to the bottom and lies in contact with the mud. It will root into the silt and soon put out new shoots.

STAR PLANTS

- *Azolla filiculoides* (fairy moss)
- *Hottonia palustris* (water violet)
- *Hydrochorus morsus-ranae* (frogbit)
- *Lagarosiphon major* (fish weed)
- *Lemna trisulca* (ivy-leaved duckweed)
- *Lobelia dortmanna* (water lobelia)
- *Myriophyllum aquaticum* (parrot's feather)
- *Nuphar lutea* (brandy bottle)
- *Nymphaea* 'Escarboucle'
- *Nymphaea* 'Gladstoneana'
- *Ranunculus fluitans* (river crowfoot)
- *Stratiotes aloides* (water soldier)

TECHNIQUE   **PLANTING WATER LILIES**

1 First line a lattice pot with hessian and then fill it with a special aquatic compost. Plant the water lily, firming it in well. Finally, place a layer of gravel on top of the compost.

2 Place the lattice pot on the first ledge of the pond so that the leaves of the water lily are lying just below the surface of the water.

3 Once the leaves have reached the surface of the water, move the pot down to the next level to stimulate further growth. Take care not to puncture the pond liner.

4 Once the leaves have again reached the surface, lower the water lily into its final deep-water position right at the bottom of the pond.

control if the whole surface is not to be covered. One or two groups of water lilies, for example, are better than a complete coverage. The same applies to other types of deep-water aquatics. In a very large pond, however, a large raft of water lilies can be very impressive.

FREE-FLOATING PLANTS

These plants float on the surface and their roots dangle beneath them, drawing nutrients from the water. Some, such as *Azolla filiculoides* and *Lemna* (duckweed), can be pests, since they can cover even a large pond in one season. Fortunately, a cold winter usually removes most of them, clearing the pond for the plants to start spreading again the following year. Free-floating plants must be kept under control, however, if any clear water is to be seen. They should not be put in a stream as they can rapidly choke the waterways. Not all are this rampant, but they should all be used cautiously as they can upset the appearance of the pond. Sometimes, in a special small pond, they can be used as sole plants to great effect. To increase them just drop a few plants in the water.

DEEP-WATER PLANTS IN STREAMS

Streams are different from ponds because the water is moving in one direction only. This flow makes it difficult for deep-water plants to gain an anchorage, and so there

are considerably fewer plants that can be grown in this situation. Some of the river crowfoots, *Ranunculus fluitans*, for example, are ideal as they not only have wonderful wavy fronds, like long tresses of hair, but are also studded with white flowers in spring and summer. Water lilies do not like such conditions. Restrict planting of streams to the margins and banks (*see pages 24–5*).

ABOVE *The flowers of this water lily are offset beautifully by the pale green, ribbed leaves of* Pistia stratiotes *(water lettuce), which is a tender floating plant.*

CREATING A MINIATURE POND

*T*here can be advantages to having small water features in a garden. Firstly, there may not be enough room for even a moderate-sized pool — construction of a pool necessitates a certain amount of upheaval and in an established garden this may not be appreciated. So a miniature pool can be an ideal alternative. Secondly, they need very little maintenance. Miniature pools, when well sited, have a decided part to play in a garden — they have a charm, elegance and simplicity that is difficult to better.

In small, intimate gardens, just a glimpse of water is all that is needed. Stuck in the middle of a bare terrace, a miniature water feature would look incongruous, but accompanied by planting in the soil around it, or by plants in pots sitting beside it, it can look delightful. Anything that will hold water can be used to create a miniature pond, but one of the best-looking and relatively cheap items is a half-barrel (*see opposite*). These can be purchased at most garden centres. Make certain that you get one that has no knot holes or other defects through which water will pour. You need one that is as natural as possible. Do not buy one that has been treated with creosote because this may kill any plants that are put into it.

LEFT *This miniature pond has been given a quirky twist by the addition of an individual water spout. Planting is been confined to the surrounds, so as not to interfere with this novel effect.*

STAR PLANTS
Eleocharis acicularis (hair grass)
Houttuynia cordata
Iris laevigata (Japanese water iris)
Juncus effusus 'Spiralis' (corkscrew rush)
Lobelia dortmanna (water lobelia)
Nymphaea 'Aurora'
Nymphaea pygmaea 'Helvola'
Nymphaea tetragona
Phragmites australis 'Variegatus' (variegated common reed)
Typha minima (dwarf reedmace)

PLANTING A HALF-BARREL POOL

It is possible to put a small fountain in a half-barrel, but it is likely to be more interesting if it is planted up. Avoid putting in too many plants, as the surface will soon become overcrowded. It is important from the visual point of view that at least half of the water surface can be seen. If plants grow too large — so that the whole surface of the water is covered — remove the plants and split them up or replace them with smaller ones. Limit the number of different plants to two or three. An ideal combination would be a round-leafed floating plant such as a miniature water lily and a vertical one like *Phragmites australis* 'Variegatus'.

A more ambitious planting can be achieved around the outside of the pond. Plants for this area can be planted directly into the ground if the pond is on or near a bed, or in pots if it is on a terrace or patio. These should

PROJECT   **CREATING A HALF-BARREL POOL**

1 If the barrel leaks, place hessian sacks around the inside and base and pour water over them. Keep them wet until the wooden staves swell up and the barrel becomes watertight. Remove the sacks.

2 Place the barrel in its final position and use a hosepipe to fill it with water right up to within 10cm (4in) of the rim. Leave the water to stand and check for any leaks.

3 Line a lattice pot with hessian and then fill it with compost. Plant a blue *Iris laevigata* into it in the normal way, and firm it in thoroughly.

4 Place this on one side of the barrel on a half brick to bring the top within 10cm (4in) of the water surface. Set another pot, containing *Nymphaea tetragona* (white pygmy water lily), in the centre.

5 Once the barrel is completely planted up, top it up with water to within 10cm (4in) of the top of the barrel.

6 Around the barrel, place other pots containing plants that associate well with water. Avoid bright colours and opt primarily for foliage plants such as hostas and ferns.

primarily be foliage plants, but avoid putting them too close to the barrel or the water will be hidden. On the other hand, do not plant them too far from the pond so that they are dissociated from it; a degree of overhanging and merging is required. Do not use tall plants in front of the pond, but place them behind it to form a backdrop. Ferns and hostas are ideal plants for this job.

USING A DUSTBIN LID

Another simple idea is to use a galvanized dustbin lid, preferably one of the larger ones. This can be sunk into the soil and decorated with a couple of rounded stones or large pebbles rather than plants. Make sure that the bottom is covered with smaller stones, then you can fill it with water. Low-growing plants can be added to the pool you have created, but as it is fairly shallow there are only a few plants that you can choose from. The real value of the galvanized dustbin lid is in its reflective surface, as it picks up the shapes of any plants that are planted around it in the surrounding soil. Some of these look good tumbling over the edge to break it up, but do not swamp it with these plantings, or let it become over-crowded. Make sure that you keep the area free of weeds. Try using *Alchemilla mollis*, *Iris ensata*, *Houttuynia*, hostas and ferns around the edges.

PLANTING THE MARGINS OF A POND

*A*part from water lilies, marginal plants such as reeds and irises are probably the plants that people most associate with water. The main reason is that they are generally much more interesting than other water plants: they are more 'three-dimensional' than floating plants, giving height as well as width, and there is a larger range of leaf shapes, flower types and colours. There are relatively few species and varieties to choose from, however, so they must be used carefully to create a pleasing design.

In the wild, marginal plants grow in the mud around the edges of ponds and in any other areas of shallow of water that may occur within them. Indeed as a pond silts up so the marginals begin to move across the whole pond. Often the floor at the edge of the pond gently slopes down into deeper water, even if the actual banks are vertical. Different plants exploit these varying depths of water. For example, *Veronica beccabunga* (brooklime) grows in the very shallow water and mud on the edge of the pool, while *Typha latifolia* (bulrush) will grow in 45cm (18in) or more of water. In a garden pond, it is possible to slope the floor of the pond to get the same effect, but pots are likely to fall

STAR PLANTS	
Acorus calamus (sweet flag)	*Iris pseudacorus* (yellow flag)
Alisma plantago-aquatica (water plantain)	*Juncus effusus* 'Spiralis' (corkscrew rush)
Butomus umbellatus (flowering rush)	*Pontederia cordata* (pickerel weed)
Caltha palustris (bog arum)	*Veronica beccabunga* (brooklime)
Iris laevigata (Japanese water iris)	*Zantedeschia aethiopica* (arum lily)

over on these slopes, so gardeners usually create a series of ledges around the pond at different depths. With preformed liners, these ledges are already built in. If, however, you create a natural pond with a 'puddled' clay liner, then the sides can be sloped and the plants inserted directly into the clay.

THE RANGE OF MARGINAL PLANTS

The number of attractive plants that will grow in shallow water is relatively small, although in the case of some of them, and irises in particular, there are many different cultivars in a range of leaf shapes and flower types and colours. Marginals vary considerably in height and shape. *Houttuynia cordata* and *Myosotis scorpioides* (water forget-me-not) are both low, spreading plants, while the irises grow tall and upright. Whatever their height, most marginals need the water to warm up before they can flower. The

LEFT Gunnera manicata *(giant rhubarb) is a stunning architectural plant for growing* beside water, but it needs a large garden to accommodate its massive proportions.

TECHNIQUE	CREATING MUDDY LEDGES

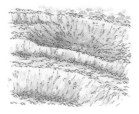

1 When excavating the hole for the pond, cut some extra narrow ledges in a few places around the perimeter. These should be dish-shaped.

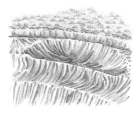

2 Spread the liner over the edge of the pond, into the dish-shaped ledge and then bring it back up to the same height as the rest of the pond surrounds.

3 Bury the edge of the liner, then fill the ledge with soil and plant into it. Plant by hand rather than with a trowel, since the latter may puncture the liner.

4 Fill the pond with water. The level will rise above the inner wall and shallowly fill the ledge, but the inner wall will prevent soil from washing into the pond.

one notable exception to this is *Caltha palustris* (marsh marigold), which flowers in the spring. It is worth including for this very reason, since nothing much else is happening at that time of the year.

As well as their visual appeal, marginal plants also provide shelter for a number of a pond's inhabitants and are used as perches and resting places by birds and insects such as dragonflies. They also provide a relatively safe haven for fish and amphibians, away from the prying eyes of herons and grass snakes (*see pages 52–3*).

DESIGNING WITH MARGINALS

Marginal plants are used visually for a variety of purposes. They break up the physical shape of the pond by hiding the banks. This may be a disadvantage in a more formal pond, but in more natural-looking ponds it gives an informal feeling to the design. It also makes the pond seem larger because its limits cannot be seen. Marginals also break up the horizontal lines of the banks, which tend to be flat. The varying heights of the plants also make the edge of the pond more interesting. Try to balance the various types of foliage plants so that there is a contrast between them. Some marginals are very invasive. Do not use *Typha latifolia* (bulrush) or *Phragmites australis* 'Variegatus' (variegated common reed) unless you have a very large pond.

In many respects, the planting of plants in shallow water is not that different from planting on land. The same principles of design apply; for example, try to use colours harmoniously and do not bury low-growing plants in the middle of taller ones where they will not be seen.

POND WILDLIFE

There are two types of wildlife in a pond. The first is introduced wildlife, which includes fish, ducks and geese. The second is the kind that finds its own way to the pond. This includes birds, dragonflies and amphibians such as frogs and toads. Whichever type you have in your pond, the only way that you will persuade them to stay is to provide them with a suitable habitat. This means you must create an inviting place with a balance of clean water, shelter and food. Most of these requirements can be met by using plants.

Most wildlife is not fussy about the appearance of the pond, but gardeners want more than a pond full of weeds and uninteresting plants. The good news is that is possible to create an area that is not only aesthetically pleasing, but also a perfect environment for wildlife.

POND PLANTS
Most of the plants that are likely to be used in and around the pond are suitable for wildlife. Some may be a bit too suitable. Ducks, for example, love to eat the overwintering buds of *Sagittaria sagittifolia* (arrow head), and they can reduce shore-planted bergenias to tatters. In the pond, under-surface plants are important as oxygenators; they also provide food for fish as well as shelter and hiding places for a wide range of pond creatures. Shelter is also provided by floating plants — both from the hot sun and from overhead predators, such as herons. They are also often the landing pads for small birds and insects. Marginal plants

provide shelter under water and are used for a variety of other purposes above water. Dragonflies use them to lay eggs on, and for safe places to dry their wings when they emerge. These plants also provide a sheltering for animals to enter the water, and, in larger ponds, for birds to nest in. On the banks the plants again act as shelters, nesting sites and perching places for birds and small mammals. A balance of all these different types of plants should be used.

CREATING AN ISLAND
A way of providing a predator-free refuge for birds is to create an island. Foxes and cats can swim but they are reluctant to do so unless really pressed. An island can be built at the time of constructing the pond, or can be added later. The pond has to be quite large for an island to work — in a smaller pond a floating island is more sensible. An island can be erected using sandbags to create a surrounding wall that is then filled with soil. If a liner is in place it will need protecting to prevent it from being pierced. A soft inner-liner covered with paving slabs is usually sufficient.

LEFT *One of the joys of water gardening is to watch the wildlife that is attracted to the pond. Here a frog takes a rest in a clump of* Lysimachia nummularia *(creeping jenny).*

MAKING AND PLANTING A FLOATING ISLAND

1 Make a frame by fixing (with galvanized nails) four pieces of 15 x 5cm (6 x 2in) wood together. Nail pieces of 10 x 2.5cm (4 x 1in) wood across these, to form a platform.

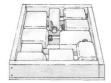

2 Turn the platform upside down and fill the 'box' with blocks of polystyrene and empty plastic containers with their lids firmly screwed on to make them watertight.

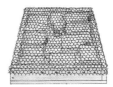

3 Nail a galvanized wire-netting over this to prevent the buoyancy material from falling out. Turn the platform back the other way up again.

4 Tie a piece of polypropylene rope just over the depth of the pond to the raft, tying the other end to a block of stone. Wrap underlay around the weight.

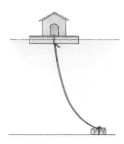

5 A duck house can be added to the platform at this point if desired. Launch the raft into its position and use the weight as its anchor.

6 To plant around the island, line a lattice pot with hessian, fill it with special aquatic compost, and plant *Pontederia cordata* (pickerel weed) in it.

7 Push the pot right down between the slats on the raft near one edge so that the plant will hang over the edge as well as across the raft when it grows.

8 Cut several shoots from a willow about 45cm (18in) long. Tie them with waterproof string to the raft so that they are vertical and the bottom 15cm (6in) are in water.

The island itself can be surrounded by marginal plants if it is not too deep. If sandbags have been used, plants such as *Caltha palustris* (marsh marigold), can be planted directly into the walls as their roots will help to bind the sacks together. Vertical plants, such as reeds and irises, look good planted in drifts against the horizontal nature of the island. They also provide height to screen the island off, giving it privacy. If the sides are steep, or the water level is likely to drop in summer, then a ramp or slope should be included to allow non-swimming birds access to the water.

FLOATING ISLANDS

A simpler form of island suitable for smaller ponds can be created by anchoring a buoyant pallet or similar structure to a large stone in the bottom of the pond. Such an island is not elegant, but the birds will love it. It can also be made to look more attractive by planting it up with a variety of marginal plants. Place the plants in lattice pots and then attach them to the raft. Willow (*Salix*) will also grow between the slats of the raft to provide cover as well as helping to disguise the structure.

BOG GARDENS

A bog garden is a useful adjunct to a pond as it enables the gardener to extend the range of plants grown around the pond. Pond liners are very efficient in keeping water in the pond, but this is to the detriment of plants that live on the nearby bank so a special wet area needs to be constructed for them. Bog gardens do not have be allied to a pond — they can be built as a separate feature without the necessity of having open water. They make interesting features in their own right, and provide a habitat for moisture-loving plants.

Bog gardens that have been built beside ponds are dealt with elsewhere (*see pages 26–7*), so we are more concerned here with bog gardens that are not necessarily associated directly with open water. In essence, these bog gardens are ordinary borders or beds except that they have been constructed in such as way as to contain soil that is kept moist all the year round. This allows a range of plants to be grown that would soon wilt and probably die under normal border conditions. It should be emphasized that many of these plants like a moist soil, not a waterlogged one, so such a bed is slightly more complicated than a basin filled with a mixture of soil and water.

PROJECT	STAND-ALONE BOG GARDEN	STAR PLANTS

1 Excavate a hole 45cm (18in) deep, covering the area for the size of bog garden you require. Keep the topsoil and discard the subsoil.

2 Line the depression with a flexible pond liner (polythene will do). Puncture holes in it to allow excess water to disperse.

3 Fill the hole to three-quarters of its depth with the topsoil mixed with organic material such as leaf mould or chipped bark (avoid anything that is very rich in nitrogen).

4 Zigzag a perforated hose across the soil, so that when it is used it will moisten the whole area. Fill up the rest of the area with soil.

5 Leave the area to settle, preferably over winter, and then top up with further soil. Plant up in spring in the conventional way.

6 If the bog garden is large, place paving slabs at intervals across the area, to enable easy access to all parts of the garden.

STAR PLANTS

- *Aruncus dioicus* (goat's beard)
- *Astilbe* x *arendsii*
- *Caltha palustris* (marsh marigold)
- *Cardamine pratensis* (cuckoo flower)
- *Eupatorium purpureum* (Joe Pye weed)
- *Euphorbia palustris* (marsh spurge)
- *Filipendula ulmaria* (meadowsweet)
- *Gunnera manicata* (giant rhubarb)
- *Hemerocallis* (day lilies)
- *Hosta sieboldiana* var. *elegans*
- *Iris ensata* (Japanese iris)
- *Primula japonica*
- *Rheum palmatum* 'Atrosanguineum' (ornamental rhubarb)
- *Trollius europaeus* (globeflower)

PLANNING AND CONSTRUCTING

Bog gardens tend to be as wide as they are long so the majority of them are round, square or broadly rectangular. The planting is likely to be informal, so the outline of the bed should similarly be informal, preferably with sinuous lines. It helps if the bog garden merges into the rest of the garden, as it should be seen as a natural feature rather than a formal one. Its size depends on many things: the overall size of the garden, the amount of plants you want to grow and the amount of time you can spend tending it.

To construct your bog garden, excavate a hole over the area to the depth of about 45cm (18in), keeping the topsoil but discarding any subsoil. Line the hole with a flexible liner. You should puncture a few holes in the bottom of the liner to allow excess water to drain away. Fill the liner with good-quality topsoil mixed with plenty of humus (avoid manure; use leaf mould or peat substitutes such as coir). The result should be a soil that holds moisture, but allows any free water to drain away. Top-dress with leaf mould or composted bark (*see opposite for further details*).

PLANTING THE BOG GARDEN

A wide range of plants will grow in a bog garden. Those that grow naturally in bogs but are also attractive are relatively small in number, so such a garden usually also includes mainly woodland plants and shade-lovers. These will grow in the open as long as they have plenty of moisture around their roots. Hostas are a good example.

Foliage can be the backbone of the bog garden, but there are also many flowering plants that can be used. Not much will flower in the winter (although willow stems are

ABOVE *A bog garden beside a pond extends the area in which you can grow moisture-loving plants, creating a special place that differs from the rest of the garden while still enhancing it.*

attractive at that time of year), but from early spring onwards *Caltha palustris* (marsh marigold) and the various cardamines will add colour. You can then have constant colour as well as foliage attraction right into autumn.

MAINTENANCE

Once the bog garden is constructed and planted, it is important to keep it moist. Use a perforated hose to supply a constant trickle of water to the soil. The hose need not be left on all the time – just long enough to keep the soil moist. It is unlikely to be needed in winter or in periods of extensive rain. The moist soil and atmosphere that will be created are perfect for the growth of weeds, mosses and algae. Although some gardeners like the moss, all three of these things will eventually become a nuisance, so keep on top of them by constant weeding.

WATCHPOINTS

- If the soil is a clay one, there is no need for a liner, but replace all the excavated clay with good-quality topsoil.
- Dig a drain, away from the hole in the clay, so that it does not act as a sump and fill with water.
- Select trees and shrubs carefully for a bog garden since not all like wet conditions.
- Keep on top of the weeds, as they like the moist conditions and will take over the entire area if they are not rigorously checked and dealt with.

PLANTING ON THE BANKS

W hile most of the planting associated with a pond is water-based, there are other plants that can be grown on the dry land next to water. These are ordinary garden plants, but they do have a particular visual affinity with water. In many respects, any garden plant can be planted near a pond, but some will create a better impact than others. Sometimes single plants can be used, while in other settings a grouping will be more appropriate. The physical treatment of these plants is no different from when they are placed elsewhere in the garden, but the overall effect will vary.

The soil surrounding a pond is often as dry as the rest of the garden. This is because the liner has done its job and kept the water in the pool. Therefore any soil in an area around a pond that you wish to plant in will need to be thoroughly prepared, and have plenty of well-rotted organic material incorporated into it. This will not only provide plenty of nutrients for the plants but will also help to preserve the moisture around their roots.

The physical planting of plants near ponds is the same as in any other part of the garden. The best time for planting them is during the spring. Plants grown in containers can be planted out later, but you will need to make sure you water them regularly until established. Once the plants are in place, the surface should be mulched, but be careful that mulch does not fall into the pond, especially if you have used farmyard manure as this will pollute the water. Do not mulch right up to the bank – leave a protective gap.

STAR PLANTS	
Alchemilla mollis	*Phyllostachys nigra*
Aruncus dioicus	*Pleioblastus auricomus*
Athyrium filix-femina	*Polystichum setiferum*
Gunnera manicata	*Rheum palmatum*
Hemerocallis	*Rodgersia aesculifolia*

There are some plants ideal for planting on the edge of the pond to soften the edge. This helps to disguise any liner that might be showing, but it also breaks up the line of the bank, making the whole area more informal. This is a much more natural effect, as, in the wild, plants often tumble down the bank and trail into water. Using plants along the edge in this way also creates a kind of timeless and tranquil quality. One of the best plants for this is

| **TECHNIQUE** | **PLANTING IN A PONDSIDE BANK** |

1 Prepare the ground by removing all perennial weeds and adding compost. Do not disturb the ground immediately next to the pond or you may puncture the liner.

2 Plant out the plants in spring to the same depth as they were in their pots. For dense plantings, place them closer together than is usually recommended.

3 Mulch between the plants to help preserve moisture and to keep weeds down. Do not drop mulch into the pond, and keep a strip next to it bare to prevent mulch being knocked or blown in.

TECHNIQUE | **GROUPING PLANTS BESIDE A POND**

1 Start by planting a group of bamboos to create the background, perhaps bringing it right round to the edge of the pond so that it is not in a straight line.

2 Plant a birch, *Betula pendula*, at the open end to give more height, and fill the middle distance with *Aruncus dioicus* and *Hemerocallis* (day lily).

3 Finally, plant the front of the border along the edge with *Alchemilla mollis* and hostas. This will break up the line along the bank and make the planting look natural.

Alchemilla mollis. This is fairly low-growing but other plants, such as some of the willows, can be used, and their branches will sweep down to the water's surface.

SINGLE PLANTS AND GROUPINGS

A solitary plant can create a good effect next to a pond. For example, a birch tree (*Betula*) near the bank or even set back a little way in a lawn will complement the pond perfectly, both in the summer when it is in leaf and in the winter with its filigree silhouette. It is best seen from the far side of the pond so that both its own shape and its reflection can be appreciated. It is best to use strong shapes in this type of planting. For example, try placing a single upright tree or a large clump of *Gunnera manicata* (giant rhubarb) or *Rheum palmatum* (ornamental rhubarb).

Plants can also be used together in groups. On the whole it is best to stick to plants that go well with water rather than, for example, using brash bedding plants. Try to use plants that look good beside water, so that it seems almost as if it is their natural home. For example, clumps of bamboos make excellent waterside plants. This is because both their movement and rustling sound seem to echo the water itself. Most ferns like a moist position, but are woodland, rather than waterside, plants. They will often grow well beside water, however, especially if the soil is full of humus and there is some shade provided by the neighbouring plants. There are also plenty of flowering

ABOVE *When planning your planting, think about how the plants will look from the other side of the pond. This use of colour is dramatic, especially when reflected in the water.*

plants that are excellent in this position, such as *Aruncus dioicus*, with its foaming creamy flower heads, or the similar-flowered rodgersias. Whatever you decide to plant, build up the overall picture by placing the lower ones beside the bank and the taller ones further back so that they can all be appreciated as a group from across the water.

SAFE WATER GARDENS FOR CHILDREN

Water gardens are as attractive and intriguing to children as they are to the adults who create them. The problem is that young children do not realize that hazards lie below the surface. Any area of open water is a potential danger to children; even small troughs of water are large enough to drown in. One drastic solution is to omit any water features from the garden; it is possible, however, to have a safe water garden, without any dangerous standing water, that can be enjoyed by all the family.

A water feature without any significant depth of water can be created by placing a reservoir below ground, out of harm's way, and restricting any above-ground water to a mere trickle. This can be provided by a water spout or a bubble fountain, where the water literally bubbles out of the ground, or by some other form of fountain. It is essential that any hidden reservoir is completely safe. A solid metal grid placed over the top of it is the safest method. The grid should be galvanized to prevent any rusting. A wooden grid can be used for a small area such as a barrel, but make sure that this is made of a hardwood or a marine ply so that it will not decay. Untreated soft wood could

STAR PLANTS
🍃 *Adiantum venustum*
🍃 *Ajuga reptans* (bugle)
🍃 *Athyrium filix-femina* (lady fern)
🍃 *Gunnera manicata* (giant rhubarb)
🍃 *Hosta crispula*
🍃 *Houttuynia cordata* 'Chameleon'
🍃 *Iris chrysographes*
🍃 *Matteuccia struthiopteris* (shuttlecock fern)
🍃 *Mimulus luteus* (monkey musk)
🍃 *Pleioblastus auricomus* (kamuro-zasa)

rot and suddenly collapse, making the area dangerous. Because the reservoir is completely covered, it means that access to it for maintenance is not easy, so whatever feature you put in will have to be able to be taken apart to let you get at the pump. This is one good reason for restricting the surface decoration to pebbles and a small millstone that can easily be lifted off. Another reason for keeping the millstone small is that the water pouring over its edges should fall within the limits of the container below.

SUITABLE FOUNTAINS

Any fountain can be used, but one with a fine spray looks best. Alternatively, a bubble fountain or a water spout can be used, so that the water falls onto a bed of pebbles or into a trough or sink filled with pebbles. With each of these features, the water falls onto the surrounding stones and

LEFT *These delightful bubble fountains have been designed to resemble sea urchins. Such enclosed water features represent a safe and fun way of including water in the garden without any fear of harm coming to the children.*

PROJECT | **MILLSTONE BUBBLE FOUNTAIN**

1 Excavate a hole where the fountain is to be positioned. Then place a wide dustbin, polythene box or other water-proof container in the hole.

2 Place the pump in the container, standing it on one or more bricks. Fill it with water and adjust the rate of flow to produce a bubbling of water only.

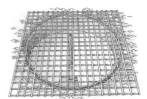

3 Cover the container with a galvanized metal grid, which you can purchase from most builders' merchants. It is essential that this grid is very strong.

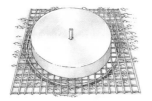

4 Place a small imitation millstone (widely available from garden and water centres) on the grid, with the nozzle from the pump passing through it.

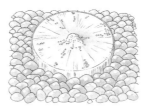

5 Place large pebbles all around the millstone to cover and hide the grid. Vary the size and colour of the pebbles to provide added visual interest.

HINTS AND TIPS

• Never have unguarded water in a garden where young children play.
• Fence off an existing water feature, using an unclimbable fence.
• If young children will be around for several years, fill in an existing pond or turn it into a sandpit and re-excavate it when they are older.
• Do not cover a pond with a plastic net and hope for the best.

quickly disappears into the hidden reservoir. In these cases, it is the stones, glistening with water and providing reflections, that create most of the visual interest.

With such small features, it is often best to keep the planting simple. Foliage plants look really good, with perhaps just a touch of colour from a long-flowering plant such as a yellow mimulus. Large-leaved plants, like hostas and ferns, are perfect, especially if the water occasionally splashes off the stones onto the foliage, making them move and glisten. The atmosphere in areas around fountains is often very moist and humid, especially if they are situated near walls. Foliage plants love these conditions and will grow well in them. Mosses are likely to appear and add to the lush effect. A few vertical plants can be used to contrast with the larger leaves.

CHILDREN AND PLANTS

Children do not see plants as aesthetic objects, but as things to play with. If you have an existing open pond that you want to make 'childproof', remove any tall plants that could screen what your child is doing. Some plants can be fun as long as they are not too near the water. *Gunnera manicata* (giant rhubarb) makes a wonderful playhouse when mature. There are some plants best avoided, however: some of the grasses, such as *Cortaderia*, have very sharp edges and the sap from euphorbias can cause skin complaints.

If your children are likely to play with the trickling water in a bubble fountain, then move any planting back or it will become damaged. As long as you are careful, both you and your children can enjoy the addition of a safe, beautiful, planted water feature.

3

THE PLANT DIRECTORY

Many water-garden plants are unusual in that they cannot be grown anywhere other than in water, but there are also many familiar plants that can be used around the edges of a pool. This mixture of plants is what makes water gardening exciting, but it can also be bewildering. The special water plants may be unfamiliar, while the others are grown out of normal context. This section will provide all the information you need to select and grow the right plants.

LEFT *Including a water feature in your garden means that you can grow a variety of interesting plants that would otherwise not survive.*

HOW TO USE THIS DIRECTORY

The Plant Directory lists all the plants that are featured in this book, together with a selection of other plants that are suitable for use in a water garden. It is not intended to be exhaustive, and experienced gardeners will have their own favourites. However, this listing has been made with the specific requirements of a water garden in mind and will guide the beginner to a range of attractive and readily available plants, shrubs and trees with which to create a beautiful water garden. Complete information on planting and maintaining the plants is given for each entry.

The Plant Directory is divided into different categories that group similar plants together. This will make it easier to select a balance of different types of plant to create your water garden. The categories are divided up as follows: submerged plants *(pages 64–5)*, floating plants *(pages 66–7)*, deep-water plants *(pages 68–9)*, water lilies *(pages 70–3)*, marginal plants *(pages 74–81)*, bog and moist soil plants *(pages 82–93)*, plants for drier banks *(pages 94–7)*, ferns

(pages 98–9), grasses and bamboos *(pages 100–3)*, and shrubs and trees *(pages 104–7)*.

The symbols panel accompanying each entry gives essential information on the growing conditions *(see opposite for a key to the symbols)*. The text next to each colour photograph gives a brief description that includes an indication of when flowering plants are in flower and advice on the preferred depth of water for each plant.

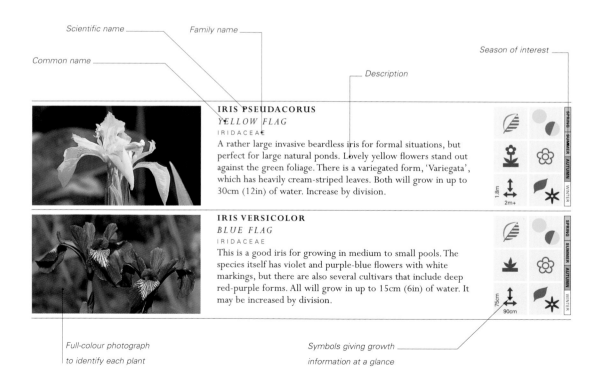

Scientific name

Family name

Common name

Season of interest

Description

IRIS PSEUDACORUS
YELLOW FLAG
IRIDACEAE
A rather large invasive beardless iris for formal situations, but perfect for large natural ponds. Lovely yellow flowers stand out against the green foliage. There is a variegated form, 'Variegata', which has heavily cream-striped leaves. Both will grow in up to 30cm (12in) of water. Increase by division.

IRIS VERSICOLOR
BLUE FLAG
IRIDACEAE
This is a good iris for growing in medium to small pools. The species itself has violet and purple-blue flowers with white markings, but there are also several cultivars that include deep red-purple forms. All will grow in up to 15cm (6in) of water. It may be increased by division.

Full-colour photograph
to identify each plant

Symbols giving growth
information at a glance

KEY TO THE SYMBOLS

 EASY TO GROW

These are tolerant plants that require no special care or conditions in order to flourish.

 MODERATE TO GROW

These are plants that require some special care, such as protection from frost.

 DIFFICULT TO GROW

These are plants that require a great deal of specialized care, and offer a challenge for the more experienced gardener.

 EVERGREEN

 SEMI-EVERGREEN

 DECIDUOUS

Deciduous plants lose all their leaves in autumn (sometimes in summer) while evergreen plants keep their foliage all the year round. Plants described as semi-evergreen may keep some or all of their foliage through the winter in sheltered gardens or if the weather is mild.

 FEATURE LEAVES OR BARK

 FEATURE SCENT

 FEATURE FLOWER

 FEATURE FRUIT

These symbols indicate the main feature of interest for each plant in the directory. This will help you to choose plants that have complementary features, or plants that will perform a specific function in your garden. The symbols show the main feature of interest, but this is not necessarily the plant's only attractive asset.

 RAPID GROWTH

 MODERATE GROWTH

 SLOW GROWTH

Speed of growth, like ease of growth, is a highly subjective category, and will vary according to local conditions. Rapid growth indicates plants that reach their full extent in a single season or plants that make substantial progress towards filling the space allowed for them in a single season. Slow growth indicates plants that take several seasons to reach their ultimate size. Moderate growth refers therefore to rates of progress between these two extremes.

The period of the year when a plant is likely to be at its most attractive is also indicated. This will allow you, for instance, to create a planting scheme that will have something of interest for each season of the year.

 HEIGHT AND SPREAD

The size of plants will vary according to the growing conditions in your garden, so these measurements are a rough guide only. In most cases the measurements refer to the size of plants and trees when mature. However, for deep-water plants and waterlilies, the vertical measurement is not their height but rather the maximum depth of water they will grow in. There are a number of entries that have been given a spread of '2m+' – this indicates that they will continue spreading until they are stopped (it does not necessarily mean that they are invasive).

 FULL SUN

 PARTIAL SUN

 SHADE

An indication of light preference is given to show each plant's optimum growing situation. Here again, this is only a rough guide, as some plants that prefer sun may also be reasonably tolerant of shade.

SUBMERGED PLANTS

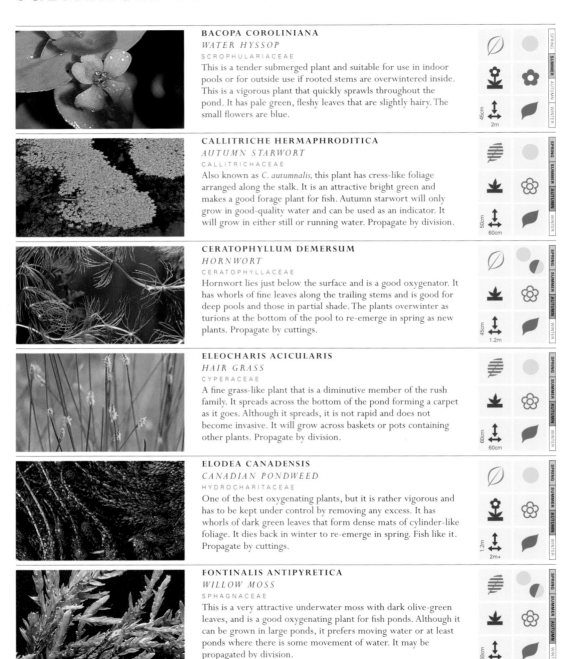

BACOPA COROLINIANA
WATER HYSSOP
SCROPHULARIACEAE

This is a tender submerged plant and suitable for use in indoor pools or for outside use if rooted stems are overwintered inside. This is a vigorous plant that quickly sprawls throughout the pond. It has pale green, fleshy leaves that are slightly hairy. The small flowers are blue.

CALLITRICHE HERMAPHRODITICA
AUTUMN STARWORT
CALLITRICHACEAE

Also known as *C. autumnalis*, this plant has cress-like foliage arranged along the stalk. It is an attractive bright green and makes a good forage plant for fish. Autumn starwort will only grow in good-quality water and can be used as an indicator. It will grow in either still or running water. Propagate by division.

CERATOPHYLLUM DEMERSUM
HORNWORT
CERATOPHYLLACEAE

Hornwort lies just below the surface and is a good oxygenator. It has whorls of fine leaves along the trailing stems and is good for deep pools and those in partial shade. The plants overwinter as turions at the bottom of the pool to re-emerge in spring as new plants. Propagate by cuttings.

ELEOCHARIS ACICULARIS
HAIR GRASS
CYPERACEAE

A fine grass-like plant that is a diminutive member of the rush family. It spreads across the bottom of the pond forming a carpet as it goes. Although it spreads, it is not rapid and does not become invasive. It will grow across baskets or pots containing other plants. Propagate by division.

ELODEA CANADENSIS
CANADIAN PONDWEED
HYDROCHARITACEAE

One of the best oxygenating plants, but it is rather vigorous and has to be kept under control by removing any excess. It has whorls of dark green leaves that form dense mats of cylinder-like foliage. It dies back in winter to re-emerge in spring. Fish like it. Propagate by cuttings.

FONTINALIS ANTIPYRETICA
WILLOW MOSS
SPHAGNACEAE

This is a very attractive underwater moss with dark olive-green leaves, and is a good oxygenating plant for fish ponds. Although it can be grown in large ponds, it prefers moving water or at least ponds where there is some movement of water. It may be propagated by division.

 leaf type  light preference  speed of growth ease of growth

HOTTONIA PALUSTRIS
WATER VIOLET
PRIMULACEAE

A very attractive plant that has bright green finely divided foliage that emerges on stout stems in spring. This is followed by long stems of pale mauve flowers carried above the surface of the water. Do not introduce to new pools until their second year. Increase by dividing the winter-resting buds (turions).

LAGAROSIPHON MAJOR
FISH WEED
HYDROCHARITACEAE

Also known as *Elodea crispa,* this looks very similar to *Elodea canadensis* (Canadian pondweed). It has whorls of dark green leaves that form a tight mass on the surface. Although it is one of the best oxygenators, it needs to be kept under control by removing excess plants. Increase by cuttings.

LOBELIA DORTMANNA
WATER LOBELIA
CAMPANULACEAE

This is a submerged aquatic that does well in shallow water and is suitable for small pools and tubs. It has dark green foliage that spreads out, forming a carpet across the bottom of the pool. It produces thin stems above the water carrying lilac flowers. It can be increased by division.

MYRIOPHYLLUM AQUATICUM
PARROT'S FEATHER
HALORAGACEAE

Also known as *M. proserpinacoides,* this is a beautiful oxygenator with long stems of soft foliage forming underwater feathery 'Christmas trees' which sometimes poke up through the surface. The leaves turn red in autumn. It will creep out of the water when overcrowded. Increase by cuttings.

MYRIOPHYLLUM SPICATUM
SPIKED MILFOIL
HALORAGACEAE

This plant has finer-cut foliage than its relative *M. aquaticum* (parrot's feather). It is bronze green in colour, and unlike its relative it is totally submerged except for the spikes of tiny red and off-white flowers that emerge in summer. It is a good plant for fish ponds, and may be propagated by cuttings.

POTAMOGETON CRISPUS
CURLED PONDWEED
POTAMOGETONACEAE

A very beautiful oxygenator which has long trails of translucent seaweed-like leaves. The leaves are bronze-green with noticeably crimpled or curled margins. It will grow in shade. The foliage becomes brittle in late summer so it is increased by cuttings taken in spring or early summer.

 height and spread   ✳ feature of interest   season of interest   *SUBMERGED PLANTS* **B – P**

FLOATING PLANTS

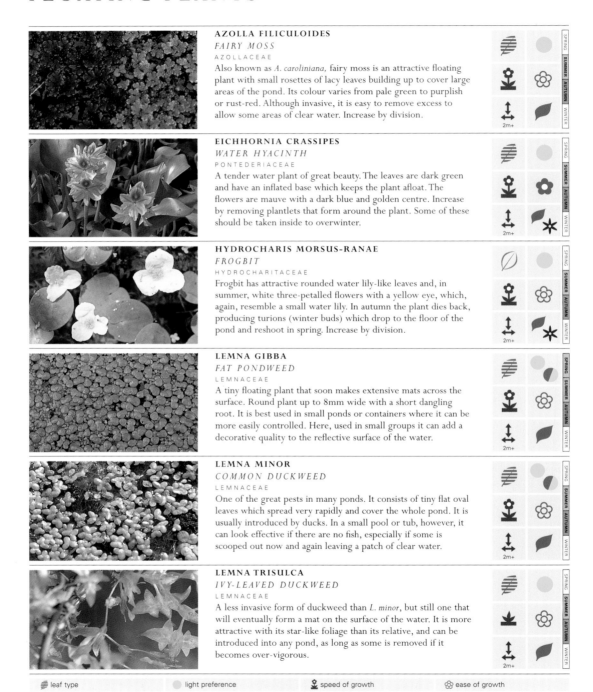

AZOLLA FILICULOIDES
FAIRY MOSS
AZOLLACEAE
Also known as *A. caroliniana,* fairy moss is an attractive floating plant with small rosettes of lacy leaves building up to cover large areas of the pond. Its colour varies from pale green to purplish or rust-red. Although invasive, it is easy to remove excess to allow some areas of clear water. Increase by division.

EICHHORNIA CRASSIPES
WATER HYACINTH
PONTEDERIACEAE
A tender water plant of great beauty. The leaves are dark green and have an inflated base which keeps the plant afloat. The flowers are mauve with a dark blue and golden centre. Increase by removing plantlets that form around the plant. Some of these should be taken inside to overwinter.

HYDROCHARIS MORSUS-RANAE
FROGBIT
HYDROCHARITACEAE
Frogbit has attractive rounded water lily-like leaves and, in summer, white three-petalled flowers with a yellow eye, which, again, resemble a small water lily. In autumn the plant dies back, producing turions (winter buds) which drop to the floor of the pond and reshoot in spring. Increase by division.

LEMNA GIBBA
FAT PONDWEED
LEMNACEAE
A tiny floating plant that soon makes extensive mats across the surface. Round plant up to 8mm wide with a short dangling root. It is best used in small ponds or containers where it can be more easily controlled. Here, used in small groups it can add a decorative quality to the reflective surface of the water.

LEMNA MINOR
COMMON DUCKWEED
LEMNACEAE
One of the great pests in many ponds. It consists of tiny flat oval leaves which spread very rapidly and cover the whole pond. It is usually introduced by ducks. In a small pool or tub, however, it can look effective if there are no fish, especially if some is scooped out now and again leaving a patch of clear water.

LEMNA TRISULCA
IVY-LEAVED DUCKWEED
LEMNACEAE
A less invasive form of duckweed than *L. minor,* but still one that will eventually form a mat on the surface of the water. It is more attractive with its star-like foliage than its relative, and can be introduced into any pond, as long as some is removed if it becomes over-vigorous.

leaf type   light preference   speed of growth   ease of growth

PISTIA STRATIOTES
WATER LETTUCE

ARACEAE

A tender floating plant with very attractive foliage. The pale green leaves are ribbed and held upright in clusters in the manner of a lettuce. In warm conditions it can become invasive. In cold areas, it will be necessary to overwinter plants inside in warm conditions. Increase by division.

RANUNCULUS AQUATILIS
WATER CROWFOOT

RANUNCULACEAE

A floating buttercup with long strands of fine hair-like leaves that lie beneath the surface. On the surface they produce a few more typical buttercup three-lobed leaves. The whole forms large floating mats. In spring a myriad of white buttercup-like flowers with golden centres are produced. Increase by division.

RANUNCULUS FLUITANS
RIVER CROWFOOT

RANUNCULACEAE

Very similar to *R. aquatilis* (water crowfoot), except that whereas its relative will grow in still water, river crowfoot only grows in moving water. It has the same type of foliage, and white flowers appear in spring. It is ideal for growing in streams, especially natural ones. Increase by division.

STRATIOTES ALOIDES
WATER SOLDIER

HYDROCHARITACEAE

An intriguing plant that resembles a pineapple top floating in water. The leaves are sword-like and finely serrated. The female flowers are solitary and the male ones in clusters, both produced on different plants and both white. They produce runners on which new plants are formed. Increase by division.

TRAPA NATANS
WATER CHESTNUT

TRAPACEAE

This is one of the few annual water plants. It forms rosettes of toothed diamond-shaped leaves and in summer bears white flowers of no great merit, followed by dark brown nuts covered in spines. Collect some of these and overwinter them on soil in a bowl of water. Transplant the seedlings in spring.

UTRICULARIA VULGARIS
GREATER BLADDERWORT

LENTIBULARIACEAE

An attractive plant with very fine filigree foliage that floats in strands just below the surface. In summer they produce rising stems of golden snapdragon-like flowers. On the underwater stems are inflated pouches which catch insects and digest them. Dies back to turions which can be used for propagation.

⚓ height and spread　　　✳ feature of interest　　　▭ season of interest　　　*FLOATING PLANTS* **A – U**

DEEP-WATER PLANTS

APONOGETON DISTACHYOS
WATER HAWTHORN
APONOGETONACEAE

A plant with long oval leaves that are green but with splashes of purple. The underside is also purple. It carries white flowers over a long period from early summer. These are sweetly scented of vanilla, which carries a long way. The plant may be propagated by division.

HYDROCLEYS NYMPHOIDES
WATER POPPY
LIMNOCHARITACEAE

This plant is grown for its stunning flowers that emerge from the water in summer. They are poppy-shaped, about 5cm (2in) across, and of a wonderful yellow with an orange eye that sets off the purple stamens. It has wide oval bright green leaves. Overwinter plants in the warm. Propagate from runners.

MARSILEA MUTICA
WATER CLOVER
MARSILEACEAE

This is an intriguing plant in that it looks like a very decorative four-leaved clover, but is in fact a fern. Each leaf is composed of a pale green inner section and a darker green outer one, separated by a bronze zone. Being a fern, it is non-flowering. Overwinter it in warm conditions in colder areas. Increase by division.

NELUMBO LUTEA
WATER CHINQUAPIN
NYMPHAEACEAE

Water chinquapin is a pale yellow-flowered lotus, somewhat smaller than *N. nucifera* (sacred lotus). It has very large leaves held well above the water. It needs a hot summer to grow well and overwintering in the warm. Best for inside pools in colder areas. Increase by division.

NELUMBO 'MOMO BOTAN'
LOTUS
NYMPHAEACEAE

This cultivar is one of the smaller lotuses. The flowers are double with rose-red petals and a yellow centre. They are distributed amongst the round green leaves which are held above the water. It can be grown outside only in warmer gardens, but it is an ideal tub-pond subject and can be moved inside.

NELUMBO NUCIFERA
SACRED LOTUS
NYMPHAEACEAE

One of the most beautiful of all flowering deep-water plants. The flowers are rose-pink and can be up to 30cm (12in) across, but it needs a hot summer to flower well. There are several cultivars. It has large leaves held above the water. It may need to be overwintered in the warm. Increase by division.

leaf type   light preference   speed of growth   ease of growth

NELUMBO NUCIFERA 'ALBA GRANDIFLORA'
LOTUS

A tender lotus that is suitable for conservatory pools or for tubs that can be moved inside for the winter. Alternatively plants can be lifted from outside pool in their pots and overwintered inside. It has a white, tinted with pink, peony type flower that is up to 25cm across and large dark green, undulating leaves.

NUPHAR ADVENA
AMERICAN SPATTERDOCK
NYMPHAEACEAE

Unlike water lilies, the American spatterdock is suitable not only for deep water but also for running water. It has typical water lily rounded leaves and small but attractive globular flowers that are yellow tinted with purple. They are vigorous and not suitable for smaller pools. Increase by division.

NUPHAR JAPONICA
JAPANESE POND LILY
NYMPHAEACEAE

This is a pond-lily with oval floating leaves that are arrow-shaped at the base. Below water are other leaves which are completely arrow shaped but with wavy margins. The flowers are up to 6cm across and are spherical, the petals being a rich gold tinged with red. There is an attractive variegated form.

NUPHAR LUTEA
BRANDY BOTTLE
NYMPHAEACEAE

A very vigorous plant with rounded water lily leaves and small globular flowers. The seed pods have a bottle shape and the flowers have an alcoholic smell: hence the English name. It will grow in slow running water. It is too vigorous for small ponds but good for larger wildlife ponds. Increase by division.

NYMPHOIDES PELTATA
WATER FRINGE
MENYANTHACEAE

This is an attractive plant, somewhat resembling a small water lily with green rounded heart-shaped leaves that are mottled with maroon. The flowers are held well above the water and are bright yellow. Their common name is derived from the fact that each petal is delightfully fringed. Increase by division.

ORONTIUM AQUATICUM
GOLDEN CLUB
ARACEAE

This is an attractive plant with blue-green hosta-shaped leaves that float when it is used as a deep-water plant, or are erect and out of the water when used as a marginal. It has curious candle-like flowers with a white base and yellow top. Increase by division or from fresh seed.

 height and spread   ✴ feature of interest   ▢▢▢ season of interest   *DEEP-WATER PLANTS **A – O***

WATER LILIES

NYMPHAEA ALBA
WHITE WATER LILY
NYMPHAEACEAE

As the name suggests, the white water lily has pure white flowers, with a golden boss in the centre. They are up to 10cm (4in) across. They are held above round dark-green leaves. This is one of the parents of many of the popular water lily hybrids. It is vigorous and hardy. Increase by division.

NYMPHAEA 'AMERICAN STAR'
NYMPHAEACEAE

A striking water lily with leaves opening with a purplish mottling but eventually turning bright green. The flowers are semi-double with pointed petals of a deep rose-pink, shading to a lighter colour towards the margins. They are about 10cm (4in) across and are held well clear of the leaves. This water lily is hardy. Increase by division.

NYMPHAEA 'ARC-EN-CIEL'
NYMPHAEACEAE

This water lily is grown for its attractive leaves. They are green and the normal water lily shape, but they are delicately splashed with white as well as purple and bronze. The flowers are not produced in any quantity, but when they are they are a very pale pink, verging on white. The plant is hardy and may be propagated by division.

NYMPHAEA 'ATROPURPUREA'
NYMPHAEACEAE

The main attraction of this plant is that it is one of the darkest red water lilies. The flowers are semi-double with rounded tips to the incurving petals and up to 15cm (6in) across. The leaves are also red when they first appear, changing to green as they age. This water lily is hardy, and can be propagated by division.

NYMPHAEA 'ATTRACTION'
NYMPHAEACEAE

This is a large-flowered variety of water lily which produces semi-double flowers of a rich garnet-red, fading to white on the margins. The flowers can reach up to 25cm (10in) in diameter. It is a vigorous plant with large round leaves more suited to larger ponds. It is hardy and can be increased by division during the growing season.

NYMPHAEA 'AURORA'
CHAMELEON WATER LILY
NYMPHAEACEAE

'Aurora' is one of the water lilies that is suitable for small pools or tubs. Its name 'chameleon' comes from the fact that in bud it is cream, opens yellow and then changes further to orange and finally red. The flowers are 5cm (2in) across. The leaves are lovat green mottled with purple. Increase by division.

≡ leaf type   ● light preference   ⚘ speed of growth   ⚘ ease of growth

NYMPHAEA 'BLUE BEAUTY'
NYMPHAEACEAE

A water lily with a mass of pointed petals that are deep blue, set off by yellow stamens. The fragrant flowers are semi-double and up to 30cm (12in) across. The green leaves are relatively small. This is a variety that needs a high summer temperature for good flowering. It is frost tender. Increase by division.

NYMPHAEA 'CAROLINIANA NIVEA'
NYMPHAEACEAE

This water lily has pure white flowers, each with a colourful centre of yellow stamens. They are semi-double, cup-shaped and may reach up to 15cm (6in) in diameter. It is one of the fragrant water lilies. The foliage is pale green. It is not too vigorous and a good plant for small ponds. This is a hardy water lily, and may be propagated by division.

NYMPHAEA 'CHARLES DE MEURVILLE'
NYMPHAEACEAE

A vigorous large-flowered water lily that is suitable only for larger ponds. The flowers can reach up to 25cm (10in) in diameter in favourable conditions. The petals are a rich red that deepen with age, fading to white at the tips. The leaves are also large and are olive-green in colour. It is hardy and may be increased by division.

NYMPHAEA 'ESCARBOUCLE'
NYMPHAEACEAE

This is one of the good deep red water lilies. The flowers are semi-double, cup-shaped and have bright yellow stamens. In good conditions the flowers can become very large – up to 30cm (12in) across. They are scented. The foliage is dark green. This is a vigorous water lily, too vigorous for small ponds. It is hardy. Increase by division.

NYMPHAEA 'GLADSTONEANA'
GLADSTONE WATER LILY
NYMPHAEACEAE

A beautiful water lily with huge pure white flowers up to 30cm (12in) in diameter with a very handsome boss of golden stamens. The flowers are semi-double and star-shaped with incurving petals. The leaves are mid-green. This is a vigorous water lily for large, deep ponds. It is hardy. Increase by division.

NYMPHAEA 'GONNERE'
NYMPHAEACEAE

A truly beautiful water lily with pure white petals and golden stamens, held in a round double flower and surrounded by green sepals. The flowers are up to 20cm (8in) in diameter. It is very free-flowering. The foliage is rounded and a fresh bright green. It is a hardy water lily, and may be propagated by division.

⬍ height and spread   ✳ feature of interest   ▭▭▭▭ season of interest   *WATER LILIES* **N**

WATER LILIES

NYMPHAEA 'JAMES BRYDON'

NYMPHAEACEAE

'James Brydon' is a very individual water lily with beautiful double peony-shaped flowers. They are crimson in colour with a central orange boss of stamens. They are fragrant and up to 20cm (8in) in diameter. The round leaves are dark purple-green with splashes of darker purple or maroon. This water lily is hardy, and may be propagated by division.

NYMPHAEA 'LAYDEKERI FULGENS'

NYMPHAEACEAE

'Laydekeri Fulgens' has star-shaped flowers with bright crimson petals and red stamens. The flowers are semi-double and can reach up to 10cm (4in) in diameter. They are fragrant. The leaves are a dark green with a purple underside. It is an easy plant to grow and suitable for smaller ponds. It is hardy and may be increased by division.

NYMPHAEA 'MARLIACEA CHROMATELLA'

NYMPHAEACEAE

A distinct water lily with broad incurving petals. The cup-shaped flowers are a delightful canary-yellow with a golden boss of stamens. They are slightly scented and are up to 20cm (8in) across. The leaves are olive-green splashed with purple which fades as the leaves age. This water lily is hardy, and may be propagated by division.

NYMPHAEA 'MIDNIGHT'

NYMPHAEACEAE

As the name indicates this is a dark-coloured water lily, with flowers in a rich bluish-purple. They are star-shaped and semi-double, up to 20cm (8in) or more in diameter. The leaves are small, and dark green flecked with brown. This is a tropical variety of water lily and is therefore frost tender. It may be increased by division.

NYMPHAEA ODORATA

FRAGRANT WATER LILY

NYMPHAEACEAE

The fragrant water lily, as its name implies, has scented flowers. The petals are white and somewhat pointed, with a large golden boss of stamens in the centre. The whole flower is up to 15cm (6in) in diameter. It is hardy and has a number of varieties of which *N.o.* 'Minor' is similar but smaller. Increase by division.

NYMPHAEA 'ODORATA SULPHUREA GRANDIFLORA'

NYMPHAEACEAE

This attractive water lily has semi-double star-shaped flowers. The petals are sulphur-yellow with stamens of the same colour. The flowers are up to 15cm (6in) across and appear throughout the summer. They are fragrant. The foliage is dark green splashed with maroon. It is hardy and may be increased by division.

🍃 leaf type   ● light preference   ⚘ speed of growth   ⚙ ease of growth

NYMPHAEA 'PANAMA PACIFIC'
NYMPHAEACEAE

This is an intriguing water lily with flowers that open a bluish-purple and then become much redder as they age. Each has a wide boss of yellow stamens tipped with violet. The foliage is olive-green. This is a tropical water lily, but one of the hardiest. It needs a relatively high summer temperature to flower well. It may be propagated by division.

NYMPHAEA 'PYGMAEA HELVOLA'
NYMPHAEACEAE

This is a very small water lily suitable for a tub or small pool. It is free-flowering with beautiful yellow flowers, offset by orange stamens. The flowers are up to 4cm (1.5in) across and have pointed petals. The leaves are very small. They are rounded and mid-green mottled with purple. It is relatively hardy and may be increased by division.

NYMPHAEA 'ROSE AREY'
NYMPHAEACEAE

A beautiful semi-double star-shaped water lily with pointed petals of a rose-pink that lighten with age. They are medium-sized, being up to 15cm (6in) across, and have a very distinct aniseed fragrance. The leaves open maroon in colour and become mid-green tinged with purple as they age. It is hardy and may be increased by division.

NYMPHAEA TETRAGONA
WHITE PYGMY WATER LILY
NYMPHAEACEAE

Also known as *N.* 'Pygmaea Alba', this is one of the smallest water lilies, suitable for tubs and small pools. The single white flowers are only 2.5cm (1in) in diameter. The dark green leaves are oval in outline and purple on the underside. It is fairly hardy, and can be divided or grown from seed.

NYMPHAEA 'VIRGINALIS'
NYMPHAEACEAE

This is a very lovely water lily with pure white flowers, each with a central boss of bright yellow stamens. They are semi-double and star-shaped, and medium in size, reaching up to 15cm (6in) in diameter. The leaves are green, tinged with purple. It is hardy, and may be increased by division.

NYMPHAEA 'WILLIAM FALCONER'
NYMPHAEACEAE

One of the best dark red-flowered water lilies. The petals are a wine-red, offset beautifully by a boss of golden stamens. The flowers are cup-shaped and of medium size, up to about 10cm (4in) across. It is free-flowering and hardy. The leaves open maroon, but turn to a dark green with purple splashes as they mature. Increase by division.

↕ height and spread   ✳ feature of interest   ▭ season of interest   *WATER LILIES* **N**

MARGINAL PLANTS

ACORUS CALAMUS
SWEET FLAG
ARACEAE

This is a plant with sword-like foliage. The flowers are held in a tight spike and are greenish, appearing in spring. The whole plant has a pleasant smell about it. There is a form *A.c.* 'Variegatus' which has attractive cream-striped foliage and is often grown in preference. Grows in up to 30cm (12in) of water. Increase by division.

ALISMA PLANTAGO-AQUATICA
WATER PLANTAIN
ALISMATACEAE

Delightfully airy flowering stems arise from bright green leaves. The white flowers are small and held on thin stems in an open pyramid. They make good stems to dry. In deeper water the leaves are below the surface. Grows in up to 30cm (12in) of water. Increase from seed or by division.

BALDELLIA RANUNCULOIDES
LESSER WATER PLANTAIN
ALISMATACEAE

Not a showy plant, but a valuable one for shallow water in a natural pond. The leaves are narrow and grass-like. The flowers resemble pale pink three-petalled buttercups. This is a plant that spreads along the margins. Grows in up to 10cm (4in) of water. Increase by seed or division.

BUTOMUS UMBELLATUS
FLOWERING RUSH
BUTOMACEAE

A beautiful flowering plant with rush-like foliage and spreading heads of pink flowers, for which it is mainly grown. The foliage is long, thin and three-sided. It is bronze-green in colour. It will grow in up to 30cm (12in) of water. Increase by bulbils that appear in the flower head, or by division.

CALLA PALUSTRIS
BOG ARUM
ARACEAE

An attractive plant that is grown both for its heart-shaped leaves and its flower heads. The flowers are relatively insignificant, but they are surrounded by distinctive white spathes. It will make a large clump, and will grow in up to 30cm (12in) of water. Increase by division or from fresh seed.

CALTHA LEPTOSEPALA
MARSH MARIGOLD
RANUNCULACEAE

This is similar to *C. palustris*, except that the flowers are white. They closely resemble buttercup flowers and the heart-shaped leaves are dark green. It is good for a natural pool where it will form small mounds round the margins. It will grow in up to 15cm (6in) of water. Increase by division or from fresh seed.

 leaf type   ● light preference    speed of growth   ⊛ ease of growth

CALTHA PALUSTRIS
MARSH MARIGOLD
RANUNCULACEAE

A very beautiful plant for the spring when its golden buttercup-like flowers open, each being at least 2.5cm (1in) across and sometimes larger. The heart-shaped leaves are dark green. There is a double form, 'Flore Pleno', which is even prettier. It will grow in up to 15cm (6in) of water. Increase by division.

45cm / 45cm

CAREX PENDULA
PENDULOUS SEDGE
CYPERACEAE

A stately plant with tall coarse grass-like leaves, long arching flower stalks and greenish-brown cylindrical flower heads. It looks best planted singly, where the arching stems can be appreciated. It will grow in up to 10cm (4in) of water. Increase by division or from fresh seed.

90cm / 60cm

CAREX RIPARIA
GREATER POND SEDGE
CYPERACEAE

Greater pond sedge in itself is not particularly interesting and is invasive. However, the variegated form 'Variegata' is not only attractive but better behaved. It has long variegated grass-like foliage striped in white. It will grow in up to 10cm (4in) of water. Increase by division or from fresh seed.

90cm / 2m+

COTULA CORONOPIFOLIA
BRASS BUTTONS
ASTERACEAE

Brass buttons is an annual or short-lived perennial that is freely self-seeding. It has yellow button-like flowers that appear in summer over a light green foliage. It makes a colourful low margin plant. It will grow in up to 10cm (4in) of water. Increase by sowing seed in spring.

15cm / 30cm

CYPERUS ERAGROSTIS
PALE GALINGALE
CYPERACEAE

Also known as *C. vegetus* this plant is similar to *C. longus*, but is shorter and has an 'umbrella' of reddish-brown spikelets in late summer. The foliage is bright green. Although it grows in up to 15cm (6in) of water it will also grow in ordinary garden soil. Increase by sowing fresh seed.

60cm / 30cm

CYPERUS LONGUS
SWEET GALINGALE
CYPERACEAE

This plant has shiny dark green leaves that have rough margins. Its other common name, 'umbrella plant', comes from its umbels of brown flowers produced mainly in late summer and early autumn. It will grow in up to 15cm (6in) of water. It may be increased by sowing fresh seed.

1.5m / 2m+

⤓ height and spread   ✳ feature of interest   ▭▭▭▭ season of interest   *MARGINAL PLANTS* **A – C**

MARGINAL PLANTS

ERIOPHORUM ANGUSTIFOLIUM
COTTON GRASS
CYPERACEAE

This is a very simple but spectacular plant. The foliage is not very impressive, but the tufts of white cotton wool that are attached to the seed as a method of dispersal are. They are held on arching rush-like stems. It must have acid conditions, and will grow in up to 15cm (6in) of water. Increase by division.

GALAX URCEOLATA
WANDFLOWER
DIAPENSIACEAE

This is a woodland plant that likes a shady position and woodland-type soil, but it will grow down to the mud margins of the pond. It has round shiny leaves which pack together to form a dense carpet. In autumn they turn red. In late spring or early summer it produces airy spikes of tiny white flowers.

GLYCERIA MAXIMA VAR. VARIEGATA
VARIEGATED MANNA GRASS
GRAMINEAE

Also known as *G. aquatica variegata*, this is a very attractive grass that can be grown in water, but it can be very invasive. It has broad grass-like leaves up to 75cm (30in) long, which are green with cream stripes. The colour does best in light shade. It will grow in up to 30cm (12in) of water. Increase by division.

HOUTTUYNIA CORDATA
SAURURACEAE

This is a charming plant with relatively large dark green leaves in a distinctive heart shape. It produces white flowers which show up well against the leaves, and is especially good for shadier situations. It spreads rapidly to form a carpet, but is rarely a nuisance. It will grow in up to 5cm (2in) of water. It may be increased by division.

HOUTTUYNIA CORDATA 'CHAMELEON'
SAURURACEAE

This plant is similar to the species, except that it has beautifully variegated foliage with red, cream and yellow added to the base colour of dark green. Although it also grows in shade, the colours glow better in full sun. It produces white flowers in spring. It will grow in up to 5cm (2in) of water. It may be increased by division.

HYPERICUM ELODES
MARSH ST JOHN'S WORT
CLUSIACEAE

A low plant that is useful for carpeting along the edges of ponds. It has green leaves that are covered in white down when they are above water, and golden-yellow saucer-shaped flowers that are borne throughout summer. It will grow in up to 10cm (4in) of water. Increase by division.

leaf type | light preference | speed of growth | ease of growth

IRIS LAEVIGATA
JAPANESE WATER IRIS
IRIDACEAE

A beautiful water iris of which the species has violet-blue flowers and a yellow throat. There are many cultivars with shades of purple and white. The flowers appear in early summer. The foliage is sword-like as in any typical iris. It will grow in up to 10cm (4in) of water. Increase by dividing the rhizomes.

IRIS PSEUDACORUS
YELLOW FLAG
IRIDACEAE

A rather large invasive beardless iris for formal situations, but perfect for large natural ponds. Lovely yellow flowers stand out against the green foliage. There is a variegated form, 'Variegata', which has heavily cream-striped leaves. Both will grow in up to 30cm (12in) of water. Increase by division.

IRIS VERSICOLOR
BLUE FLAG
IRIDACEAE

This is a good iris for growing in medium to small pools. The species itself has violet and purple-blue flowers with white markings, but there are also several cultivars that include deep red-purple forms. All will grow in up to 15cm (6in) of water. It may be increased by division.

JUNCUS EFFUSUS
SOFT RUSH
JUNCACEAE

The soft rush is perfect for a pond that requires a natural look. It grows in large tufts of dark green cylindrical leaves. Tufts of brown flowers appear in summer. It self-sows and can become mildly invasive. It will grow in up to 15cm (6in) or more of water. Increase by division.

JUNCUS EFFUSUS 'SPIRALIS'
CORKSCREW RUSH
JUNCACEAE

This is a curiosity rather than a beautiful plant. It is a form of the soft rush in which the stems have become twisted into loose spirals. It is more suitable for a smaller pond than the species and is not so invasive. It will grow in up to 15cm (6in) of water. It may be increased by division.

LUDWIGIA PALUSTRIS
WATER PURSLANE
ONAGRACEAE

Most plants in this genus come from warm regions, but this is hardy. It is a plant for natural ponds with weak stems that grow upright in water but creep along in mud. The green leaves are oval, and it has insignificant green petalless flowers. It will grow in up to 30cm (12in) of water. Increase by division.

⬍ height and spread   ✳ feature of interest   ▭▭▭ season of interest   *MARGINAL PLANTS* **E – L**

MARGINAL PLANTS

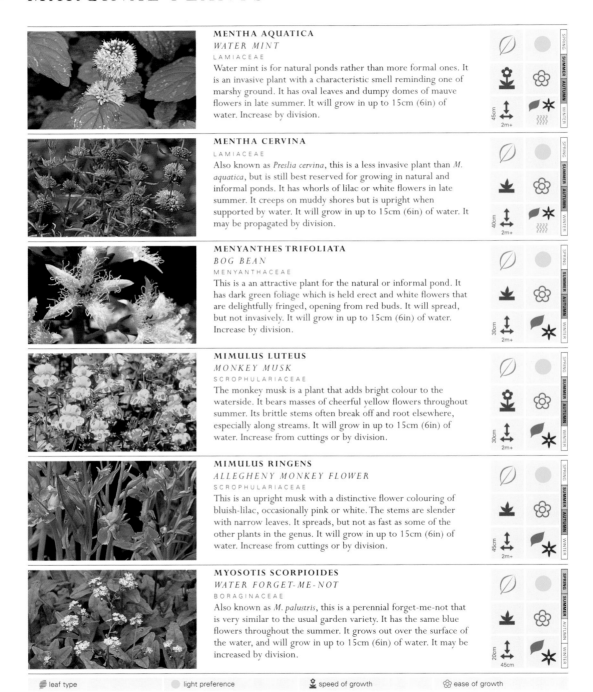

MENTHA AQUATICA
WATER MINT
LAMIACEAE

Water mint is for natural ponds rather than more formal ones. It is an invasive plant with a characteristic smell reminding one of marshy ground. It has oval leaves and dumpy domes of mauve flowers in late summer. It will grow in up to 15cm (6in) of water. Increase by division.

MENTHA CERVINA
LAMIACEAE

Also known as *Preslia cervina*, this is a less invasive plant than *M. aquatica*, but is still best reserved for growing in natural and informal ponds. It has whorls of lilac or white flowers in late summer. It creeps on muddy shores but is upright when supported by water. It will grow in up to 15cm (6in) of water. It may be propagated by division.

MENYANTHES TRIFOLIATA
BOG BEAN
MENYANTHACEAE

This is a an attractive plant for the natural or informal pond. It has dark green foliage which is held erect and white flowers that are delightfully fringed, opening from red buds. It will spread, but not invasively. It will grow in up to 15cm (6in) of water. Increase by division.

MIMULUS LUTEUS
MONKEY MUSK
SCROPHULARIACEAE

The monkey musk is a plant that adds bright colour to the waterside. It bears masses of cheerful yellow flowers throughout summer. Its brittle stems often break off and root elsewhere, especially along streams. It will grow in up to 15cm (6in) of water. Increase from cuttings or by division.

MIMULUS RINGENS
ALLEGHENY MONKEY FLOWER
SCROPHULARIACEAE

This is an upright musk with a distinctive flower colouring of bluish-lilac, occasionally pink or white. The stems are slender with narrow leaves. It spreads, but not as fast as some of the other plants in the genus. It will grow in up to 15cm (6in) of water. Increase from cuttings or by division.

MYOSOTIS SCORPIOIDES
WATER FORGET-ME-NOT
BORAGINACEAE

Also known as *M. palustris*, this is a perennial forget-me-not that is very similar to the usual garden variety. It has the same blue flowers throughout the summer. It grows out over the surface of the water, and will grow in up to 15cm (6in) of water. It may be increased by division.

leaf type   light preference   speed of growth   ease of growth

NARTHECIUM OSSIFRAGUM
BOG ASPHODEL
MELANTHIACEAE

This small plant is insignificant when it is not flowering. In summer, when in flower, however, the spikes of golden stars stand out strikingly against their background. It is a plant of either shallow water or boggy ground. It will grow in up to 5cm (2in) of water. Increase by division.

PELTANDRA SAGITTIFOLIA
ARROW ARUM
ARACEAE

Also known as *P. alba*, this plant is grown mainly as a foliage plant. It forms clumps of typical arrow-shaped arum leaves which are held well above the water. Its flowers are white spathes, sometimes followed by red berries. It will grow in up to 15cm (6in) of water. Increase by division.

PHRAGMITES AUSTRALIS 'VARIEGATUS'
VARIEGATED COMMON REED
POACEAE

The species is only really suitable for very large ponds, but this variegated form is not quite as invasive and can be used in smaller situations. It has arching leaves with golden-yellow stripes. Its flowers are plumes of purple. It will grow in up to 90cm (36in) of water. Increase by division.

PONTEDERIA CORDATA
PICKEREL WEED
PONTEDERIACEAE

Pickerel weed is one of the most attractive marginal plants. It has shiny green spear-shaped leaves which cover the surface of the water, and held above them over a long season are spikes of deep blue flowers. It will grow in up to 30cm (12in) of water. Increase by division.

RANUNCULUS FLAMMULA
LESSER SPEARWORT
RANUNCULACEAE

Not as spectacular as *R. lingua*, this spearwort has a quiet presence that makes it useful for growing among other marginals in a natural pond. Its golden buttercup-like flowers shine out among the other plants over a long season. It will grow in up to 30cm (12in) of water. Increase by division.

RANUNCULUS LINGUA
GREATER SPEARWORT
RANUNCULACEAE

This is more of a garden-worthy plant than *R. flammula*, but is still best used in a natural pond, particularly where it can grow among other plants. It has narrow leaves and large golden buttercup flowers. It will grow in up to 30cm (12in) of water. It may be increased by division.

⬍ height and spread   ✳ feature of interest   ▭▭▭ season of interest   *MARGINAL PLANTS* **M – R**

MARGINAL PLANTS

RUMEX HYDROLAPATHUM
WATER DOCK
POLYGONACEAE

Docks are normally kept out of the garden, but the water dock is a good plant for a natural pond. It has broad coarse leaves and spires of green flowers that turn red in seed. The foliage takes on red autumn tints. It will grow in up to 30cm (12in) of water. Increase by division.

SAGITTARIA SAGITTIFOLIA
ARROW HEAD
ALISMATACEAE

Also known as *S. japonica*, this will make large clumps if allowed to, which makes it more suitable to a natural pond than a formal one. The foliage is arrow-shaped and is held well above the water, complemented by airy stems of white flowers. It will grow in up to 30cm (12in) of water. Increase by division.

SAGITTARIA SAGITTIFOLIA 'FLORE PLENO'
ARROW HEAD
ALISMATACEAE

While the species (*see above*) is more for the wild garden, this is a choice plant for more formal conditions, especially if it is kept under control. The attraction is the whorls of fluffy double white flowers carried on tall spikes. It will grow in up to 30cm (12in) of water. Increase by division.

SAURURUS CERNUUS
LIZARD'S TAIL
SAURURACEAE

An unusual plant with bright green heart-shaped leaves over which hang the lizards' tails of the name: creamy-white flowers nodding in long sprays. They have the bonus of being scented. This plant can be grown in small pools. It will grow in up to 30cm (12in) of water. Increase by division.

SCHOENOPLECTUS LACUSTRIS SUBSP. TABERNAEMONTANI 'ALBESCENS'
CYPERACEAE

This is one of the stateliest of rushes, and is sometimes listed under *Scirpus lacustris*. It forms tall clumps of yellowish white foliage striped along its length with green. It brightens up a dull corner. The flowers are brown spikelets. It will grow in up to 15cm (6in) of water. Increase by division.

SCHOENOPLECTUS LACUSTRIS SUBSP. TABERNAEMONTANI 'ZEBRINUS'
ZEBRA RUSH
CYPERACEAE

This plant is very similar to the related cultivar 'Albescens' (*see above*), except in one important visual way: the whitish stripes go round the stems rather than along their length. It makes a very eye-catching plant. It will grow in up to 15cm (6in) of water. Increase by division.

🌿 leaf type   ● light preference   🌱 speed of growth   ❀ ease of growth

SPARGANIUM ERECTUM
BRANCHED BUR-REED
SPARGANIACEAE

Also known as *S. ramosum*, this is one of those plants that are perfect for adding to the diversity of a wildlife pond but not decorative enough for more formal situations. Its main feature is the green fruiting burrs. It will grow in up to 15cm (6in) of water. Increase by division.

TYPHA ANGUSTIFOLIA
NARROW-LEAVED REEDMACE
TYPHACEAE

Sometimes known as the lesser bulrush, this plant is a more elegant form of its larger relative; but it is still rather invasive and must be kept under control in smaller ponds. It has the typical brown cylindrical seed heads, so good for drying. It will grow in up to 60cm (2ft) of water. Increase by division.

TYPHA LATIFOLIA
BULRUSH
TYPHACEAE

This plant is unsuitable for anything but the largest ponds. Here it will create drifts making an impressive sight. Its progress in smaller pools can be curtailed by pulling out the excess. The brown cylindrical seed heads are very attractive. It will grow in up to 60cm (2ft) of water. Increase by division.

TYPHA MINIMA
DWARF REEDMACE
TYPHACEAE

This is the smallest member of the genus, and since it is not only smaller but also less invasive can be grown with effect in smaller ponds, and even in tubs. The leaves are thin and the seed head more rounded than in the other plants. It will grow in up to 30cm (12in) of water. Increase by division.

VERONICA BECCABUNGA
BROOKLIME
SCROPHULARIACEAE

This is a delightful plant, a little reminiscent of a forget-me-not with starry blue flowers with white eyes held in spikes among and above the glossy foliage. It is only for shallower water of up to 10cm (4in) or so, and will also grow in the bank-side mud. Increase by division.

ZANTEDESCHIA AETHIOPICA
ARUM LILY
ARACEAE

One of the most attractive of all waterside species, with its large dark green leaves topped by elegant pure white spathes. Some forms are tender, but if grown under water that does not freeze solid they are hardy. It will grow in up to 30cm (12in) of water. Increase by division.

⬍ height and spread   ✳ feature of interest   ▭▭▭ season of interest   *MARGINAL PLANTS* **R – Z**

BOG AND MOIST-SOIL PLANTS

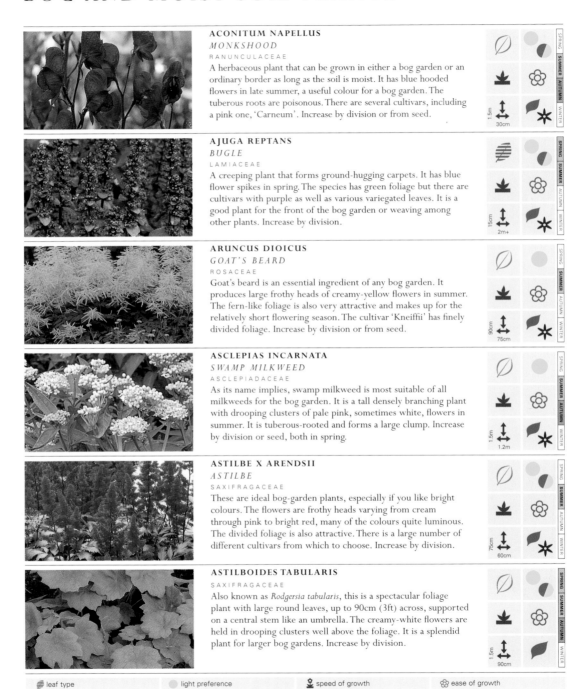

ACONITUM NAPELLUS
MONKSHOOD
RANUNCULACEAE

A herbaceous plant that can be grown in either a bog garden or an ordinary border as long as the soil is moist. It has blue hooded flowers in late summer, a useful colour for a bog garden. The tuberous roots are poisonous. There are several cultivars, including a pink one, 'Carneum'. Increase by division or from seed.

AJUGA REPTANS
BUGLE
LAMIACEAE

A creeping plant that forms ground-hugging carpets. It has blue flower spikes. The species has green foliage but there are cultivars with purple as well as various variegated leaves. It is a good plant for the front of the bog garden or weaving among other plants. Increase by division.

ARUNCUS DIOICUS
GOAT'S BEARD
ROSACEAE

Goat's beard is an essential ingredient of any bog garden. It produces large frothy heads of creamy-yellow flowers in summer. The fern-like foliage is also very attractive and makes up for the relatively short flowering season. The cultivar 'Kneiffii' has finely divided foliage. Increase by division or from seed.

ASCLEPIAS INCARNATA
SWAMP MILKWEED
ASCLEPIADACEAE

As its name implies, swamp milkweed is most suitable of all milkweeds for the bog garden. It is a tall densely branching plant with drooping clusters of pale pink, sometimes white, flowers in summer. It is tuberous-rooted and forms a large clump. Increase by division or seed, both in spring.

ASTILBE X ARENDSII
ASTILBE
SAXIFRAGACEAE

These are ideal bog-garden plants, especially if you like bright colours. The flowers are frothy heads varying from cream through pink to bright red, many of the colours quite luminous. The divided foliage is also attractive. There is a large number of different cultivars from which to choose. Increase by division.

ASTILBOIDES TABULARIS
SAXIFRAGACEAE

Also known as *Rodgersia tabularis*, this is a spectacular foliage plant with large round leaves, up to 90cm (3ft) across, supported on a central stem like an umbrella. The creamy-white flowers are held in drooping clusters well above the foliage. It is a splendid plant for larger bog gardens. Increase by division.

leaf type   light preference   speed of growth   ease of growth

ASTRANTIA MAJOR
MASTERWORT
APIACEAE

Astrantias give a bog garden a cool, elegant touch. The flowers are whitish-green, and these last for a long time. There are also pink and red forms including the wine-red 'Ruby Wedding'. The foliage plays an important part, with 'Sunningdale Variegated' having cream-splashed leaves. Increase by division or seed.

60cm / 45cm

CARDAMINE PRATENSIS
CUCKOO FLOWER
BRASSICACEAE

The cuckoo flower is one of the joys of springtime in the bog garden. It is a slim elegant plant with delightful fresh-looking lilac flowers. When suited it can spread, but is rarely a nuisance. There are several double-flowered forms of which 'Flore Pleno' is the best. Increase from seed.

45cm / 23cm

CHELONE OBLIQUA
TURTLEHEAD
SCROPHULARIACEAE

This is a valuable plant in that it flowers late, carrying the flowers in stubby spikes. They are hooded, tubular and rose-pink. Earlier in the season, the leaves are attractive enough for it to act as a foliage plant. *C. glabra* is a similar white species. It can be increased either by division or from seed.

90cm / 45cm

CIMICIFUGA SIMPLEX
BUGBANE
RANUNCULACEAE

The bugbanes make wonderful bog plants with their towering spires of white flowers borne in autumn. The foliage is also attractive, and is purple in some varieties. There is a number of other species and cultivars worth looking at. It can be increased by division or from seed.

1.8m / 60cm

DARMERA PELTATA
UMBRELLA PLANT
SAXIFRAGACEAE

Also known as *Peltiphyllum peltatum*, in spring this plant produces naked stems, up to 45cm (18in) high, topped with a dome of pink flowers. As the flowers fade, large round leaves, 30cm (12in) across, appear. Their thick rhizomes spread to make quite a forest. It is increased by division.

90cm / 2m+

DODECATHEON MEADIA
SHOOTING STARS
PRIMULACEAE

An attractive low-flowering plant with glossy foliage, from which in late spring naked stems carry whorls of pink, purple or white flowers that hang down. Their petals are reflexed and they look very much like shooting stars. There are other species of equal beauty. Increase from seed or by division.

45cm / 25cm

 height and spread   ✳ feature of interest   ▢ season of interest   *BOG/MOIST-SOIL PLANTS **A – D***

BOG AND MOIST-SOIL PLANTS

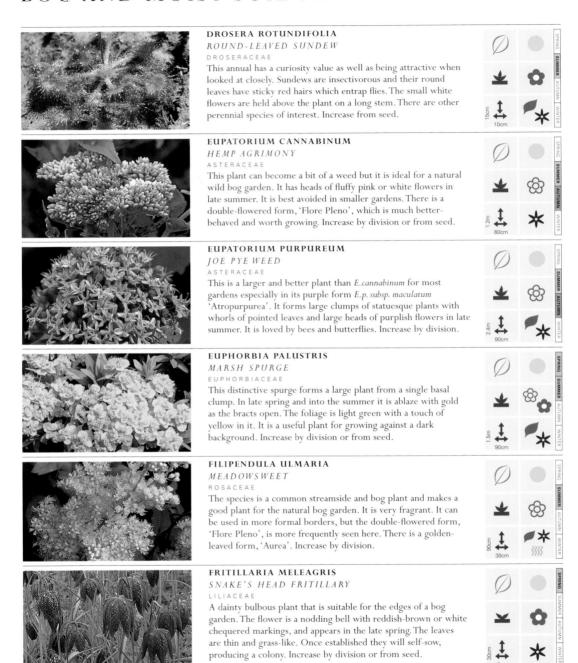

DROSERA ROTUNDIFOLIA
ROUND-LEAVED SUNDEW
DROSERACEAE
This annual has a curiosity value as well as being attractive when looked at closely. Sundews are insectivorous and their round leaves have sticky red hairs which entrap flies. The small white flowers are held above the plant on a long stem. There are other perennial species of interest. Increase from seed.

EUPATORIUM CANNABINUM
HEMP AGRIMONY
ASTERACEAE
This plant can become a bit of a weed but it is ideal for a natural wild bog garden. It has heads of fluffy pink or white flowers in late summer. It is best avoided in smaller gardens. There is a double-flowered form, 'Flore Pleno', which is much better-behaved and worth growing. Increase by division or from seed.

EUPATORIUM PURPUREUM
JOE PYE WEED
ASTERACEAE
This is a larger and better plant than *E.cannabinum* for most gardens especially in its purple form *E.p. subsp. maculatum* 'Atropurpurea'. It forms large clumps of statuesque plants with whorls of pointed leaves and large heads of purplish flowers in late summer. It is loved by bees and butterflies. Increase by division.

EUPHORBIA PALUSTRIS
MARSH SPURGE
EUPHORBIACEAE
This distinctive spurge forms a large plant from a single basal clump. In late spring and into the summer it is ablaze with gold as the bracts open. The foliage is light green with a touch of yellow in it. It is a useful plant for growing against a dark background. Increase by division or from seed.

FILIPENDULA ULMARIA
MEADOWSWEET
ROSACEAE
The species is a common streamside and bog plant and makes a good plant for the natural bog garden. It is very fragrant. It can be used in more formal borders, but the double-flowered form, 'Flore Pleno', is more frequently seen here. There is a golden-leaved form, 'Aurea'. Increase by division.

FRITILLARIA MELEAGRIS
SNAKE'S HEAD FRITILLARY
LILIACEAE
A dainty bulbous plant that is suitable for the edges of a bog garden. The flower is a nodding bell with reddish-brown or white chequered markings, and appears in the late spring. The leaves are thin and grass-like. Once established they will self-sow, producing a colony. Increase by division or from seed.

leaf type   light preference   speed of growth   ease of growth

GENTIANA ASCLEPIADEA
WILLOW GENTIAN
GENTIANACEAE

A graceful plant that is well worth its place in a bog garden. It has arching stems with rows of upward-facing gentian-blue flowers, above the bright green willow-like leaves. They form a non-spreading clump although some forms self-seed. There is a white form, *G.s.* var. *alba*. Increase from seed.

75cm / 90cm

GEUM RIVALE
WATER AVENS
ROSACEAE

A pretty little plant with pendulous flowers that are rose pink in colour. The species is well worth growing, but there are several cultivars, such as 'Leonard's Variety', that are even better, especially for a more formal garden. Ensure that they are not swamped by other plants. Increase by division.

30cm / 30cm

GUNNERA MAGELLANICA
GUNNERACEAE

A complete contrast to *G. manicata*, this is a very low creeping plant, growing no more than 7.5cm (3in) tall, that carpets the ground with deep green leaves. In summer these are topped by short spikes of red flowers. It is slightly tender and may need winter protection. Increase by division.

7.5cm / 45cm

GUNNERA MANICATA
GIANT RHUBARB
GUNNERACEAE

A giant among herbaceous plants with enormous rhubarb-like leaves over 2m (7ft) wide, held on thick stems covered with prickles. The green flower heads are curiously cone-shaped. This is a plant only for those gardens that have space. It needs winter protection of a cover of leaves. Increase by division.

2.5m / 3m

HEMEROCALLIS FULVA
DAY LILY
HEMEROCALLIDACEAE

Each flower only lasts a day, but there is a constant supply of them. The flowers are very similar to lilies, mainly based on yellow and brown colours, and it has a fountain of strap-like leaves. There are thousands of day lily hybrids to choose from, most suitable for the bog garden. Increase by division.

1.5m / 90cm

HOSTA CRISPULA
HOSTACEAE

This is a decoratively leaved hosta with pointed oval leaves that are mainly dark green, except for the margins which are variegated with white. The lilac flowers are lily-shaped and are carried on a spike in summer. Hostas can fall prey to slugs and snails. Avoid windy sites. Increase by division.

75cm / 45cm

⬍ height and spread   ✱ feature of interest   ▭▭▭▭ season of interest   *BOG/MOIST-SOIL PLANTS* **D – H**

85

BOG AND MOIST-SOIL PLANTS

HOSTA FORTUNEI VAR. ALBOPICTA F. AUREA
HOSTACEAE

This is a delightfully attractive hosta with golden-coloured foliage turning gradually pale green as summer progresses. The leaves are spear-shaped and textured with parallel veins. It is an excellent foliage plant for brightening up a dark corner or growing against a dark background. The flower spikes carry lilac flowers. Increase by division.

HOSTA 'FRANCES WILLIAMS'
HOSTACEAE

This plant is typical of the group of hostas with golden variegation. It has roundish leaves with a puckered texture. They are bluish-green in the centre with an irregular margin of yellow. There are many other varieties where the green and yellow colourings are reversed. The flowers are pale lavender. It may be increased by division.

HOSTA SIEBOLDIANA VAR. ELEGANS
HOSTACEAE

A very beautiful hosta with large-heart shaped leaves that are blue and heavily textured with deep veins. The tall spikes of lily-like flowers are produced in late summer and are pale mauve. When grown in moist soil, this is a good plant for sun or shade. Guard against slugs. Increase by division.

IMPATIENS GLANDULIFERA
POLICEMAN'S HELMET
BALSAMINACEAE

Also known as *I. roylei*, the common name relates to the curious shape of the pink flowers, which do indeed look like helmets. It is an attractive tall fast-growing annual that rapidly spreads by seed. It can be too vigorous for a small garden. Do not plant by a natural stream as the plant will spread downstream.

IRIS ENSATA
JAPANESE IRIS
IRIDACEAE

Also known as *I. kaempferi*, this is an attractive iris that has given rise to a large number of cultivars and hybrids. The species has purple flowers, but the colours of the forms vary considerably and include white. The sword-like leaves have a prominent midrib. Increase by division.

IRIS ORIENTALIS
TURKISH IRIS
IRIDACEAE

Also known as *I. ochroleuca*, this is a good tall form of iris with strong upright stems and foliage. The flowers are clear white with yellow blotches on the lower petals, which make them stand out among other vegetation. It spreads gently but not invasively. Increase by division.

 leaf type    light preference    speed of growth   ease of growth

IRIS SIBIRICA
SIBERIAN FLAG
IRIDACEAE

A group of very useful and beautiful plants for the bog garden with narrow leaves and blue or purple flowers. There is a range of over a hundred cultivars and hybrids (known as Siberian hybrids) with variations on these colours as well as yellow, white, pink and red. Increase by division after flowering.

LEUCOJUM AESTIVUM
SUMMER SNOWFLAKE
AMARYLLIDACEAE

In spite of its name, this is a late-winter or early-spring flower. From a distance the white flowers look like an over-large snowdrop, but they have in fact only a bell of outer petals and no inner ones. The foliage is dark green and strap-like. This bulbous plant likes to grow in damp soil. Increase by division.

LIGULARIA DENTATA
LEOPARD PLANT
ASTERACEAE

An attractive plant both for its foliage and its flowers. The former are large, heart-shaped and dark green. The flowers are bright orange and up to 5cm (2in) across. There are several cultivars, of which 'Desdemona', with its purple reverse to the leaves, is one of the best. It is a martyr to slugs. Increase by division.

LIGULARIA 'THE ROCKET'
ASTERACEAE

Unlike its relative, *L. dentata*, this plant produces tall spires of small yellow flowers, for which 'the rocket' is a good description. The plants look magnificent when grown in a large group, especially against a green or dark background. The deeply cut foliage and dark stems also add to the attraction. It may be increased by division.

LOBELIA CARDINALIS
CARDINAL FLOWER
CAMPANULACEAE

The cardinal flower is ideal for making a splash of colour in the bog garden or beside a stream. It has a basal rosette of bronze leaves from which extends a tall leafy spike of brilliant crimson flowers. In spite of looking tender, this plant is hardy. Increase from cuttings, by division or from seed.

LOBELIA X GERARDII 'VEDRARIENSIS'
CAMPANULACEAE

This is a hardy perennial lobelia that forms a non-invasive spreading clump. The large tubular flowers are carried in tall spikes and are bluish-purple. Like most lobelias, it likes a moist soil. There are a few other similar cultivars, including 'Rosencavalier', which has redder flowers. They can be increased by division or from cuttings.

⬍ height and spread   ✳ feature of interest   ▦ season of interest   *BOG/MOIST-SOIL PLANTS H – L*

BOG AND MOIST-SOIL PLANTS

LOBELIA 'QUEEN VICTORIA'

CAMPANULACEAE

There is a whole series of red lobelia hybrids, based on
L. cardinalis and other species, of which 'Queen Victoria' is one of
the best. It has brilliant red flowers and beautiful red-purple
foliage. 'Cherry Ripe', 'Dark Crusader' and 'Will Scarlet' are
other good varieties to be recommended. Protect in winter.
Increase from cuttings or by division.

LOBELIA SIPHILITICA

BLUE CARDINAL FLOWER

CAMPANULACEAE

As its common name implies, this is the blue equivalent of the
red *L. cardinalis*. The foliage is green and the clear blue flowers,
which appear in late summer, are held in spikes above a basal
rosette of leaves. This is a hardier plant than many of its relatives.
Increase from cuttings, by division or from seed.

LYCHNIS FLOS-CUCULI

RAGGED ROBIN

CARYOPHYLLACEAE

A delightful little plant that needs careful siting so that it is not
swamped by other plants. The flowers are rose-pink and are
typical of the dianthus family, except that they are deeply cut so
that they look as if they have been torn. Out of flower, the plant
is not significant. Increase from seed.

LYSICHITON AMERICANUS

YELLOW SKUNK CABBAGE

ARACEAE

An absolutely essential plant for the bog garden if you have
space. The flowers, which appear in spring, are giant hooded
yellow spathes with a green flower spike inside. They are
followed by enormous leaves that resemble a giant cos lettuce. It
needs a lot of space, and spreads. Increase from seed.

LYSICHITON CAMTSCHATCENSIS

ASIAN SKUNK CABBAGE

ARACEAE

This form from eastern Asia is similar to that found growing on
the American side of the Pacific, *L. americanus,* except that it is
smaller in all its parts and the spathe is white instead of yellow. It
is malodorous. It also needs space, but not so much. It is hardy.
Increase from seed.

LYSIMACHIA NUMMULARIA

CREEPING JENNY

PRIMULACEAE

A good ground-covering plant that forms a dense carpet of green
leaves spangled with golden cup-shaped flowers. The plant is best
known for its 'Aurea' cultivar, which has golden foliage and is
ideal for brightening up darker spots, especially between other
plants. It spreads, but not invasively. Increase by division.

---

leaf type   light preference   speed of growth   ease of growth

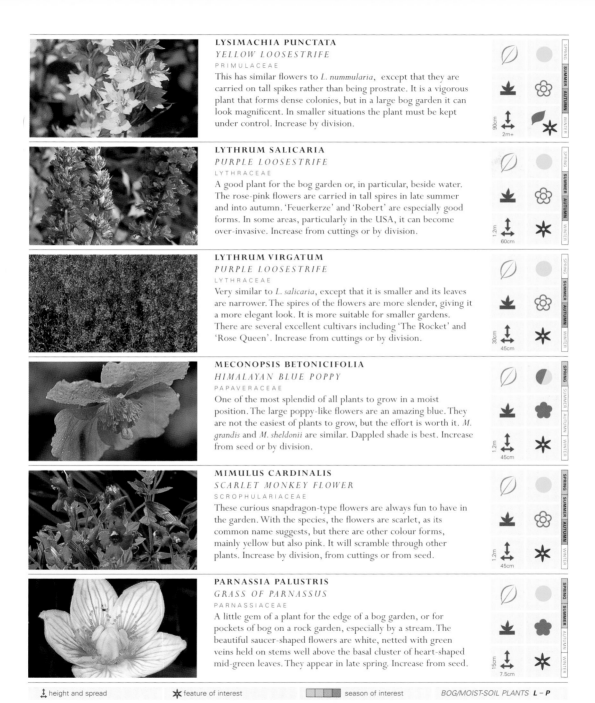

LYSIMACHIA PUNCTATA
YELLOW LOOSESTRIFE
PRIMULACEAE

This has similar flowers to *L. nummularia*, except that they are carried on tall spikes rather than being prostrate. It is a vigorous plant that forms dense colonies, but in a large bog garden it can look magnificent. In smaller situations the plant must be kept under control. Increase by division.

90cm
2m+

LYTHRUM SALICARIA
PURPLE LOOSESTRIFE
LYTHRACEAE

A good plant for the bog garden or, in particular, beside water. The rose-pink flowers are carried in tall spires in late summer and into autumn. 'Feuerkerze' and 'Robert' are especially good forms. In some areas, particularly in the USA, it can become over-invasive. Increase from cuttings or by division.

1.2m
60cm

LYTHRUM VIRGATUM
PURPLE LOOSESTRIFE
LYTHRACEAE

Very similar to *L. salicaria*, except that it is smaller and its leaves are narrower. The spires of the flowers are more slender, giving it a more elegant look. It is more suitable for smaller gardens. There are several excellent cultivars including 'The Rocket' and 'Rose Queen'. Increase from cuttings or by division.

30cm
45cm

MECONOPSIS BETONICIFOLIA
HIMALAYAN BLUE POPPY
PAPAVERACEAE

One of the most splendid of all plants to grow in a moist position. The large poppy-like flowers are an amazing blue. They are not the easiest of plants to grow, but the effort is worth it. *M. grandis* and *M. sheldonii* are similar. Dappled shade is best. Increase from seed or by division.

1.2m
45cm

MIMULUS CARDINALIS
SCARLET MONKEY FLOWER
SCROPHULARIACEAE

These curious snapdragon-type flowers are always fun to have in the garden. With the species, the flowers are scarlet, as its common name suggests, but there are other colour forms, mainly yellow but also pink. It will scramble through other plants. Increase by division, from cuttings or from seed.

1.2m
45cm

PARNASSIA PALUSTRIS
GRASS OF PARNASSUS
PARNASSIACEAE

A little gem of a plant for the edge of a bog garden, or for pockets of bog on a rock garden, especially by a stream. The beautiful saucer-shaped flowers are white, netted with green veins held on stems well above the basal cluster of heart-shaped mid-green leaves. They appear in late spring. Increase from seed.

15cm
7.5cm

⬍ height and spread   ✳ feature of interest   ▭▭▭ season of interest   *BOG/MOIST-SOIL PLANTS* **L – P**

BOG AND MOIST-SOIL PLANTS

PERSICARIA BISTORTA
BISTORT
POLYGONACEAE

A fresh-looking plant with large pale green leaves and cylindrical heads of pale pink flowers held well above the foliage. They appear in early summer, often continuing throughout summer. The best form, with large flower heads, is 'Superba', which makes good ground cover. Increase by division.

PETASITES JAPONICUS VAR. GIGANTEUS
GIANT BUTTERBUR
ASTERACEAE

This is a plant that is best avoided unless there is plenty of room, but it is quite spectacular where space does permit. The white flowers appear on cone-like flower heads in late winter. They have a wonderful sweet scent. The huge leaves are light green and round. Increase by division.

PINGUICULA GRANDIFLORA
BUTTERWORT
LENTIBULARIACEAE

Small plants for the edge of a bog garden, or in boggy pockets in a rock garden or beside a stream. They are carnivorous plants that catch insects on their sticky yellow-green leaves. The flowers are held on stems above the leaves and are rose-pink. It may be increased from seed.

PRIMULA BEESIANA
PRIMULACEAE

A delightful candelabra primula that is perfect for the bog garden or alongside a stream. The flowers are carried in whorls around the stems and are a deep rose-pink with a yellow eye. The leaves are the typical primula shape and are carried in a basal rosette with the flowers held well above them. It may be increased from seed or by division.

PRIMULA BULLEYANA
BULLEY'S PRIMULA
PRIMULACEAE

Candelabra primulas, with whorls of flowers on an extended stem held well above the leaves, are ideal for the bog garden. This one has rusty orange flowers, which are red while still in bud. A hybrid, *P. bulleesiana* provides a large range of colours, from orange to mauve. Increase from seed.

PRIMULA DENTICULATA
DRUMSTICK PRIMULA
PRIMULACEAE

A very distinctive primula with each flower head resembling a drumstick, with a ball of flowers on top of a naked stem. The typical flowers are mauve, with deep purple and white variants. The leaves are the typical primrose type that become very long after flowering. Increase from seed or by division.

 leaf type   ● light preference    speed of growth   ease of growth

PRIMULA FLORINDAE
GIANT COWSLIP
PRIMULACEAE

One of the latest primulas to flower. It has tall stems topped with a whorl of pendent bell-shaped sulphur-yellow flowers. The leaves form vigorous clumps and make good ground cover. This an excellent plant for the bog garden and waterside, especially against a dark background. Increase from fresh seed or by division.

PRIMULA JAPONICA
PRIMULACEAE

A very easy-to-grow candelabra primula, which, once established, will self-sow without becoming a nuisance. The whorls of flowers are produced in shades of pink to purple, red and white. They appear above relatively coarse vigorous leaves. 'Postford White' and 'Miller's Crimson' are two very good cultivars to be recommended. Increase by division or from seed.

PRIMULA PULVERULENTA
PRIMULACEAE

A candelabra primula that is very similar to *P. japonica*. It is rather more refined in appearance, but the main difference is that all the stems are covered in a powdery meal which gives them a whitish appearance. The flowers are rich red with purple eyes and they are 2.5cm (1in) across. It may be increased either by division or from seed.

PRIMULA ROSEA
PRIMULACEAE

This is a primula in the primrose style. It is low-growing and has typical primrose flowers appearing on single stems direct from the rosette of typical primrose leaves. The flowers are rose-pink, although there are some variants. The leaves have a purplish tinge. Increase either by division or from seed.

PRIMULA VIALII
PRIMULACEAE

This is one of the most curious-looking primulas. It is more like a hardy orchid. The buds and the flowers form a pyramid with the red buds at the top and the mauvish-pink flowers at the bottom. They are held on a tall naked stem above a cluster of normal primula leaves. It is only short-lived and will need replacing regularly from seed.

RANUNCULUS ACONITIFOLIUS
FAIR MAIDS OF KENT
RANUNCULACEAE

A delightful airy plant that is perfect for the bog garden. The branching stems carry large white buttercup-type flowers above typical dark green buttercup leaves. While the single form has a simple purity, there is a double form, 'Flore Pleno', which is just as beautiful. It is best increased by division.

---

‡ height and spread   ✳ feature of interest   ▮▮▮▮ season of interest   *BOG/MOIST-SOIL PLANTS* **P – R**

BOG AND MOIST-SOIL PLANTS

RHEUM PALMATUM
ORNAMENTAL RHUBARB
POLYGONACEAE

Ornamental rhubarb is a very dramatic plant for a bog garden, particularly when it is in flower and seed. It has huge jagged-edged leaves and great clusters of frothy cream flowers on tall stems. There are some cultivars, such as 'Atrosanguineum', that have red flowers and purple foliage. Increase by division.

RODGERSIA AESCULIFOLIA
SAXIFRAGACEAE

An essential foliage ingredient for a bog garden, this clump-forming rhizomatous perennial has palmate mid-green leaves that look very similar to those of the horsechestnut. They are pleated and have delicate bronze veins and stalks. The flowers are held above the leaves in frothy cream clusters in late summer. It is best increased by division.

RODGERSIA PINNATA
SAXIFRAGACEAE

Another clump-forming rhizomatous perennial that makes a good foliage plant for the bog garden or beside water. This one has palmate leaves, made up of pairs of opposite leaflets. In the form 'Superba' these are purple when young. It has frothy heads of pink flowers held well above the foliage. It may be increased by division.

SARRACENIA PURPUREA
PITCHER PLANT
SARRACENIACEAE

A carnivorous plant with modified leaves that create upright tubular 'pitchers' with a hood in which trapped insects are digested. These pitchers are a beautiful green and red. The drooping flowers are dark red. They are not reliably hardy. Increase by division or from seed.

SCHIZOSTYLIS COCCINEA
KAFFIR LILY
IRIDACEAE

One of the few bulbous plants suitable for the bog garden. This produces spikes of satiny flowers in the autumn and often on into winter. The flowers are different shades of pink. The leaves are strap-like and of little significance. There is a number of cultivars. It spreads but is not invasive. Increase by division.

SENECIO SMITHII
ASTERACEAE

This is a daisy-like flowering plant with white petals and a yellow central disc. The flowers are carried in large clusters above the leathery glossy leaves that are toothed down the margins. The flowers are up to 5cm (2in) across. It will grow in wet soil, even mud, and is very hardy. Increase from seed or by division.

🌿 leaf type   ⬤ light preference   ⚘ speed of growth   ⚙ ease of growth

SYMPHYTUM IBERICUM
COMFREY
BORAGINACEAE
Also known as *S. grandiflorum*, comfreys are really only for the larger garden with space for their invasive habit. This is one of the shorter forms with rough spear-shaped leaves. The flowers are produced from coils of buds and are creamy-white, tinted with blue and pink in some forms. Increase by division.

TELEKIA SPECIOSA
TELEKIA
ASTERACEAE
Also known as *Buphthalmum speciosum*, this is a tall coarse plant that is perfect for large bog gardens but too big for small beds or gardens. It produces large toothed oval leaves and golden-yellow daisy-like flowers up to 5cm (2in) across, in late summer and autumn. Increase from seed or by division.

TROLLIUS ACAULIS
DWARF GLOBEFLOWER
RANUNCULACEAE
This is the smallest of the globeflowers and is best sited in boggy areas in a rock garden or by a stream. In spite of its diminutive size, the bowl-shaped flowers are still quite large, reaching up to 5cm (2in) across. They are golden-yellow and held above fresh green foliage. Increase from seed.

TROLLIUS X CULTORUM CULTIVARS
GLOBEFLOWER
RANUNCULACEAE
This covers a large range of clump-forming perennials, which are differentiated by the colour of their flowers. These vary from very pale yellow to orange tinged with red. They are attractive plants with large flowers and good foliage. They should all be increased by division and not from seed.

TROLLIUS EUROPAEUS
GLOBEFLOWER
RANUNCULACEAE
This species is in many ways the best suited to a natural bog garden. The large globular flowers are yellow and not quite as spectacular as many of the *Trollius x cultorum* cultivars but are still worth growing. They are held well above the typical buttercup foliage. Increase either from seed or by division.

VERATRUM VIRIDE
INDIAN POKE
MELANTHIACEAE
Although several veratrums can be grown in moist soil, this one grows in marshy conditions. It is a tall plant with spreading stems, covered in star-like green flowers. It is one of the most spectacular of the green-flowered plants. It also has attractive pleated leaves. Beware slugs. Increase from seed or by division.

 height and spread ✳ feature of interest season of interest *BOG/MOIST-SOIL PLANTS* **R – V**

PLANTS FOR DRIER BANKS

ALCHEMILLA MOLLIS
LADY'S MANTLE
ROSACEAE

Lady's mantle is strictly neither a water nor a bog plant, but it is one of the most effective plants for growing next to water. It has a great froth of yellowish green flowers that flop over the bank, and lovely pleated round leaves. Cut back after flowering to promote another crop of flowers. Increase by division or from seed.

45cm / 45cm

ANEMONE X HYBRIDA
JAPANESE ANEMONE
RANUNCULACEAE

The Japanese anemone is a graceful plant that builds up into a colony and is ideal for planting beside a more formal pool. The flowers are usually pink although there are several white varieties which go especially well with water. They dislike soil that is too dry. Increase by root cuttings or careful division.

1.5m / 2m+

ANGELICA ARCHANGELICA
APIACEAE

This is a herb, but it is more frequently grown as a decorative plant. Its natural habitat is beside streams, and it certainly always looks good growing beside water. It is a statuesque plant with large, rounded heads of small greenish-yellow flowers, which look good among foliage plants. It will also grow in bog gardens. Increase from seed.

2m / 1.2m

AQUILEGIA VULGARIS
COLUMBINE
RANUCULACEAE

These delicate, blue or purple flowers grow on the edge of woodlands in the wild, but in the garden they look particularly good growing alongside streams or beside a pond as long as they are mixed with foliage plants rather than brash flowers. There are other colours to choose from. Grow from seed.

60–90cm / 45cm

ARTEMISIA LACTIFLORA
WHITE MUGWORT
ASTERACEAE

Most artemisias like dry soil and are not suitable for growing beside water. White mugwort, however, needs a moister soil and its green foliage and dark stems and frothy, creamy flowers make it an ideal waterside plant. The variety 'Guizhou' has purple-flushed leaves. Increase by division.

1.5m / 60cm

BERGENIA CORDATA
ELEPHANT'S EARS
SAXIFRAGACEAE

Wonderful plants grown for their large rounded leaves and for their pink or white flower heads. The leaves make excellent ground cover throughout the year, often taking on reddish tinges in winter. Unfortunately the leaves can be ruined by ducks eating them. There are many cultivars. Increase by division.

60cm / 75cm

leaf type | light preference | speed of growth | ease of growth

BRUNNERA MACROPHYLLA

BORAGINACEAE

A plant with heart-shaped leaves that spreads non-invasively to form a good ground cover. In spring the leaves are overtopped with sprays of blue flowers. They look particularly good in a mass sweeping down to the water's edge as long as the soil is not too waterlogged. There are white-flowered and variegated forms. Increase by division.

45cm / 60cm

CROCOSMIA 'LUCIFER'

MONTBRETIA

IRIDACEAE

The brilliant scarlet of these flowers stands out well against the sword-like leaves and is particularly good when seen across water. Even when not in flower, the stiff upright leaves make these good waterside plants. A good clump rather than extensive planting is all that is required. Increase by dividing the corms.

1.2m / 90cm

DIERAMA PULCHERRIMUM

WANDFLOWER

IRIDACEAE

A beautiful plant in which long thin stems bearing dangling purple flowers arch above strap-like leaves. It should be planted at the edge of a bog garden, preferably over water so that its grace and beauty can be easily appreciated. Do not overcrowd it. Increase from seed or by division.

1.5m / 60cm

EPILOBIUM ANGUSTIFOLIUM VAR. ALBUM

WHITE ROSEBAY WILLOWHERB

ONAGRACEAE

The ordinary rosebay willowherb is too vigorous for any garden, but the white form is much better. It will make a small colony but should not get out of hand. It has white flowers which contrast beautifully with its fresh green foliage. A large group is very satisfying by a pond. Increase by division.

1.5m / 90cm

EPIMEDIUM GRANDIFLORUM

BARRENWORT

BERBERIDACEAE

Epimediums make good ground cover with attractive leaves and airy sprays of intriguingly shaped flowers. The flower colour is mainly purple in the species, but there are white and yellow forms. It forms a large clump but is not invasive. It is good for planting beneath waterside shrubs. Increase by division.

30cm / 30cm

EUPHORBIA GRIFFITHII

EUPHORBIACEAE

An attractive spurge usually seen in its varieties 'Dixter' and 'Fireglow'. It has bright orange-red bracts which give it a sunny glow. The leaves and stems are also suffused with red, making it a striking foliage plant for a bank. In light soils it is invasive, however, spreading quickly by underground rhizomes. It may be increased by division.

90cm / 2m+

✧ height and spread   ✳ feature of interest   ▭▭▭▭ season of interest   *PLANTS – DRYER BANKS* **A – E**

PLANTS FOR DRIER BANKS

EUPHORBIA SCHILLINGII

EUPHORBIACEAE

Because of their fresh green nature, euphorbias are good plants to grow next to water – they complement the coolness beautifully. Many of the euphorbias are worth growing, but *E. shillingii* has the advantages of height and the fact that it is late-flowering. The flowers do not appear until late summer and continue into autumn. Increase by division.

INULA MAGNIFICA

ASTERACEAE

These are tall statuesque plants that add scale to the side of a pond. The flowers resemble golden-yellow daisies, and may be up to 15cm (6in) across. The leaves are large and relatively coarse, but at the same time make good foliage for bankside plants. They look best when planted on the bank behind tall marginals. They may be increased from seed.

IRIS CHRYSOGRAPHES

IRIDACEAE

This is one of the most elegant and sophisticated of all irises, and therefore should be positioned where it can be easily seen and appreciated. The flowers have the typical iris shape, but it is very refined. Their colour is very dark purple, so dark that there are some cultivars that are almost black. The lower petals have gold markings. Increase by division.

LEUCANTHEMUM VULGARE

MARGUERITE

ASTERACEAE

This simple flower is a yellow-centred white daisy, which reaches up to 5cm (2in) in diameter. The plant is not grand enough for ornamental borders, but is perfect for a meadow garden that comes down to the edge of a natural pond. Add a few plants to the grass and then let it seed around to produce more.

MIMULUS LEWISII

GREAT PURPLE MONKEY FLOWER

SCROPHULARIACEAE

The shape of these flowers is typical of that of all monkey flowers, but the colouring is more subtle – rose-pink with a yellow throat. The foliage is greyish and slightly sticky. Although like all mimulus it prefers moist soils, this one will also grow in drier conditions. Increase from seed or by division.

OPHIOPOGON PLANISCAPUS 'NIGRESCENS'

CONVALLARIACEAE

This is a small grass-like plant that is primarily grown for its black foliage. It is not a plant normally associated with ponds, but it is very good for planting in the upper part of a pebble beach where it is not so wet, especially if the pebbles are pale in colour. It has short spikes of white flowers followed by attractive shiny black seeds. Increase by division.

 leaf type   ⬤ light preference   ♨ speed of growth   ⚙ ease of growth

PHORMIUM TENAX
NEW ZEALAND FLAX
AGAVACEAE

This is a statuesque plant that really needs room to be seen. It has huge strap-like leaves that arch out like a fountain. They are a pale olive-green, but there are plenty of cultivars and hybrids with coloured and variegated foliage. The red flowers are held above these in giant sprays. Increase by division.

PRIMULA VULGARIS
PRIMROSE
PRIMULACEAE

Primroses are the epitome of spring with their posies of pale yellow flowers nestling among green leaves. One of the best positions for them is on a pondside bank, especially when they may be viewed from across the water. They go particularly well with a natural pond. Increase from seed or by division.

RANUNCULUS FICARIA
LESSER CELANDINE
RANUNCULACEAE

One of the first plants to flower in the bog garden, this has low rosettes of heart-shaped leaves over which yellow buttercup-like flowers appear on short individual stems. There are orange and white varieties as well as mottled and purple-leaved ones. It dies right back after flowering. Increase by division.

SENECIO TANGUTICUS
CHINESE GROUNDSEL
ASTERACEAE

An unusual and wonderful plant for growing beside a pond. It is tall with black stems, large jagged leaves and airy conical heads of yellow flowers that have just the right quality for this position. They clump up to form a colony, which looks better than individual plants. It needs a moist soil. Increase by division.

TROPAEOLUM MAJUS
NASTURTIUM
TROPAEOLACEAE

Annual nasturtiums make a vivid splash of colour when tumbling down a bank to the water's edge or climbing through a shrub growing out over the water. The bright reds, oranges and yellows add an exotic touch to the scene, especially when seen from across the pond. Propagate from seed.

VINCA MAJOR
GREATER PERIWINKLE
APOCYNACEAE

A herbaceous sub-shrub with cool blue flowers that spreads out across banks and even onto the water. It dies back each winter, but gradually makes a good ground cover, weaving its way through other plants. There is a form with variegated foliage that is useful for darker corners. Increase by division.

---

 height and spread   feature of interest   ▭▭▭ season of interest   *PLANTS – DRIER BANKS* **E – V**

FERNS

ADIANTUM PEDATUM
NORTHERN MAIDENHAIR FERN
ADIANTACEAE
A very attractive fern for a choice position. It has slender strap-like fronds that are divided to the central rib. The stems are black and the fronds a fresh mid-green. Together they make a delicate plant, especially in spring when the new leaves are unfurling. Increase by division or from spores.

ADIANTUM VENUSTUM
ADIANTACEAE
This is a very delicate fern with triangular fronds made up of many tiny triangular leaflets, creating a lacy effect. It is a marvellous plant to grow next to falling water, as the cascading leaflets resemble the falling drops. The dark stems also enhance the appearance. Increase by division or from spores.

ASPLENIUM SCOLOPENDRIUM
HART'S TONGUE FERN
ASPLENIACEAE
Unlike most ferns, this has undivided fronds. They are like a broad undulating tongue, ending in a point, and are mid green. There is a number of cultivars, some, especially the Crispum Group, with very attractive curled edges. They make a good contrast to plants with more frilly foliage. Increase by division or from spores.

ATHYRIUM FILIX-FEMINA
LADY FERN
WOODSIACEAE
The lady fern has beautiful much-divided fronds of a fresh light green which arch in a graceful manner. The plant should not be overcrowded, so that it can show off its shape. There are many cultivars with differing frond shapes. It self-sows, but rarely becomes a nuisance. Increase by division or from spores.

BLECHNUM SPICANT
HARD FERN
BLECHNACEAE
This is a very hardy fern that is useful for damp places with a peaty soil. It forms small clumps from which erupt narrow fronds with deep indentations. They are leathery and dark green in colour. There is also a number of interesting cultivars. Increase by division or from spores.

CYRTOMIUM FALCATUM
JAPANESE HOLLY FERN
DRYOPTERIDACEAE
An intriguing fern with broad leaflets that look very much like the holly leaves of its common name. They are arranged alternately on the stems of the frond and are a shiny dark green. This plant is not completely hardy and is only suitable for warmer areas. It can be increased either from spores or by division.

 leaf type   light preference   speed of growth   ease of growth

DRYOPTERIS DILATATA
BROAD BUCKLER FERN
DRYOPTERIDACEAE

Also known as *D. austriaca*, this is an attractive arching fern with broad much divided fronds. The leaflets are dark green and roughly triangular in shape. The stems are dark brown. There is a number of cultivars with crests or crisped margins. It can be increased either from spores or by division.

MATTEUCCIA STRUTHIOPTERIS
SHUTTLECOCK FERN
WOODSIACEAE

The shuttlecock or ostrich plume fern is one of the most attractive of all waterside ferns. In spring, the deeply divided fronds open erect with the tips curled outward, just like a giant shuttlecock. It is essential that it is planted in moist soil. It spreads by underground rhizomes. Increase by division.

ONOCLEA SENSIBILIS
SENSITIVE FERN
WOODSIACEAE

This is a fern for larger bog gardens as it spreads rapidly by underground rhizomes. It is unusual in that it sends up single fronds rather than a whole plant, thus making it good for ground cover. The fronds are deeply divided into wide leaflets. It can be easily increased by division.

OSMUNDA REGALIS
ROYAL FERN
OSMUNDACEAE

One of the largest ferns that can be grown outside in temperate areas. It is attractive at all stages, including spring when the new fronds first unfurl. It has large divided bright green leaves and leaflets which are completely brown with spores and held like flower heads in spikes. Increase by division or from spores.

POLYSTICHUM SETIFERUM
SOFT SHIELD FERN
DRYOPTERIDACEAE

The soft shield fern is a very graceful and beautiful plant with much-divided fronds. The silhouette is spear-shaped and the colour a soft mid-green. The stems are covered with shaggy brown scales. This is a good plant for a dry bank. It can be increased either by division or from spores.

WOODWARDIA RADICANS
CHAIN FERN
BLECHNACEAE

The chain fern is a wonderful sight with graceful arching stems of divided leaves. The name comes from the chains of spores to be found on the backs of the leaflets. It is slightly tender and therefore needs some winter protection in colder areas. It can be increased by pegging down the bud at the tip of the fronds.

↕ height and spread   ✱ feature of interest   ▭▭▭ season of interest   *FERNS* **A – W**

BOG-GARDEN AND WATERSIDE BAMBOOS

BAMBUSA MULTIPLEX
HEDGE BAMBOO
POACEAE

Also known as *B. glaucescens*, this is a very tall bamboo with gently arching canes that spread to form a dense clump. As its common name suggests, it makes a good hedge or windbreak. Its evergreen leaves, arranged in pairs, are each narrow and up to 15cm (6in) long. They have a silver underside. Increase by division.

CHUSQUEA CULEOU
CHILEAN BAMBOO
POACEAE

An evergreen with upright canes of glossy green, which carry papery pointed leaf sheaths that give it a distinctive and attractive appearance. The leaves are narrow and up to 10cm (4in) long. When the leaves eventually fall, the leaf stalks remain, giving the lower plant a bristly appearance. Increase by division.

PHYLLOSTACHYS BAMBUSOIDES
TIMBER BAMBOO
POACEAE

A tall evergreen that forms spreading clumps. The canes are quite thick and deep green in colour. The leaf sheaths have distinctive bristles. The leaves are a glossy dark green and up to 20cm (8in) long. 'Allgold' has golden canes and sometimes striped leaves. Increase by division.

PHYLLOSTACHYS FLEXUOSA
ZIGZAG BAMBOO
POACEAE

An evergreen that takes its common name from the fact that the ribbed stems are not straight but slightly zigzagged. The stems are green, turning to black, and they can be very tall. It has narrow leaves up to 15cm (6in) long, which retain their fresh colour throughout winter. Increase by division.

PHYLLOSTACHYS NIGRA
BLACK BAMBOO
POACEAE

This is a very beautiful bamboo which, although it spreads, is not invasive. The gracefully arching stems start out green before later turning black, and the colour is at its best in full sun. The leaves are small and mid-green. There are several interesting cultivars to choose from. Increase by division.

PLEIOBLASTUS AURICOMUS
KAMURO-ZASA
POACEAE

Also known as *Arundinaria auricoma*, this is a shorter bamboo that spreads slowly to form a large clump. Its big attraction is its broad foliage that is golden striped with green. It is evergreen, but is best cut down each spring to produce fresh foliage. Increase by division in spring.

≣ leaf type   ● light preference   ⚓ speed of growth   ⚙ ease of growth

PLEIOBLASTUS VARIEGATUS
DWARF WHITE-STRIPED BAMBOO
POACEAE

Also known as *Arundinaria fortunei* and *A. variegata*, this is a variegated bamboo with creamy-white stripes down the length of its dark leaves, which are up to 15cm (6in) long. The canes are pale green. It is neither tall nor invasive, making it a very attractive plant for the smaller garden. Increase by division.

75cm ↕ 1.2m

PSEUDOSASA JAPONICA
ARROW BAMBOO
POACEAE

One of the most commonly seen bamboos, which, although quite coarse, is worth its place as it is tough and creates good protection for other plants. It forms spreading clumps of green stems, with persistent brown sheaths. It has broad pointed evergreen leaves. Increase by dividing the rhizomes in spring.

5m ↕ 2m+

SASA VEITCHII
KUMA ZASA
POACEAE

A medium-sized bamboo that is best known for its variegated foliage during the winter months when the dark green leaves take on distinctive off-white margins. It is a hardy evergreen with pale stems and purple sheaths. It can be invasive. Increase by dividing the rhizomes in spring.

1.5m ↕ 2m+

SEMIARUNDINARIA FASTUOSA
NARIHIRA BAMBOO
POACEAE

An evergreen that forms dense spreading clumps. It is tall and upright, and useful for screens and backdrops. The attractive stems are green striped with purple, and when the papery cane sheaths open the cane is dark purple underneath. The leaves are up to 15cm (6in) long. Increase by division.

7m ↕ 2m+

SHIBATAEA KUMASASA
POACEAE

This is a low-growing evergreen bamboo which has the advantage that it does not spread invasively. The canes are short-jointed and a brownish-green in colour. The deep green leaves are relatively broad and they are up to 13cm (5in) long, making a very attractive display. It is a good bamboo for the smaller garden. Increase by division.

1.5m ↕ 60cm

YUSHANIA ANCEPS
ANCEPS BAMBOO
POACEAE

Also known as *Arundinaria anceps*, this is an attractive but invasive bamboo, which will throw up new clumps some distance from the original. The stems are tall and arch gracefully. The pointed leaves are glossy and mid-green. Increase by dividing the newly emerging clumps.

4m ↕ 2m+

 height and spread   ✳ feature of interest   ▢▢▢ season of interest   *BAMBOOS **B – Y***

BOG-GARDEN AND WATERSIDE GRASSES

ALOPECURUS PRATENSIS 'AUREOVARIEGATUS'
GOLDEN FOXTAIL GRASS
POACEAE

A variegated grass with yellow stripes down its broad leaves. It forms non-spreading clumps, which need to be cut back to the ground in spring to allow the new growth to look its best. It produces cylindrical flower heads in summer. It is suitable for growing on dry banks. Increase by division in spring.

ARUNDO DONAX
GIANT REED
POACEAE

A stately grass with very tall stems and alternate arching leaves that are blue-green in colour. It produces whitish spikelets of flowers but these are rarely seen in cooler areas. Cut back in autumn. There is a good variegated form with white stripes, known as *A.d.* var. *versicolor*. Increase by division.

CORTADERIA SELLOANA
PAMPAS GRASS
POACEAE

Pampas grasses are very majestic with their tall stems bearing white plumes arising from a fountain of narrow leaves. The leaves can be razor-sharp, so be careful when handling or weeding near them. There are sizes for all kinds of garden, and variegated cultivars include 'Gold Band' with gold stripes. They may be increased by division.

HAKONECHLOA MACRA 'AUREOLA'
POACAE

This is a low clump-forming deciduous perennial grass that spreads slowly to form mounds. It has arching leaves that are striped in bright yellow and green. The colour gradually changes to red as the season progresses. In autumn, it has attractive reddish-brown flowers held in spikes above the foliage. It can be increased by division in spring.

HORDEUM JUBATUM
SQUIRREL TAIL GRASS
POACEAE

An annual (or sometimes perennial) grass that will self-seed. It is grown for its very feathery arching flower heads, which look particularly good with the sun behind them. The silver flower head looks like water from a fountain and therefore makes a good feature on a dry bank. Increase from seed in spring.

LUZULA SYLVATICA
GREATER WOODRUSH
JUNCACEAE

This is rather a coarse sedge, but it is useful as it grows in damp shade. It has strap-like leaves with hairy margins and spikes of brown flowers. There is a cultivar 'Marginata' with white edges to the leaves. There is also another attractive species, *L. nivea*, which has sprays of whiter flowers. Increase by division.

leaf type   light preference   speed of growth   ease of growth

MISCANTHUS SINENSIS
EULALIA
POACEAE

Miscanthus is a genus of many superb perennial grasses. One of the best is *M. sinensis* and its cultivars, with their tall graceful flowering stems appearing above fountains of narrow foliage. The silky flowers appear in late summer and continue well into autumn. Increase by division in spring.

2m / 90cm

PANICUM CAPILLARE
OLD-WITCH GRASS
POACEAE

Old-witch grass is an annual grass with broad arching leaves and tufts of flowers that look like sprays of water, especially when they catch the sun. It is a medium-sized plant that forms clumps, and is good for growing on dry banks near a pond or other water feature. It can be increased from seed in spring.

90cm / 60cm

PENNISETUM ALOPECUROIDES
CHINESE FOUNTAIN GRASS
POACEAE

A very attractive plant for smaller gardens where the larger grasses are too big. It has narrow mid-green leaves forming a fountain of foliage from which arise graceful arching stems with sparse cylinders of flowers, like delicate bottle brushes. Increase by division in spring or from seed sown fresh.

90cm / 45cm

PHALARIS ARUNDINACEA VAR. PICTA
RIBBON GRASS
POACEAE

This is a very beautiful grass, but one that tends to be very invasive, so it must either be rigorously controlled or only used in a large garden with space. It is the white-striped leaves, touched with pink when young, that give this plant its beauty. There is a number of cultivars. Increase by division in spring.

90cm / 2m+

SPARTINA PECTINATA 'AUREOMARGINATA'
POACEAE

This is a grass that provides a long season of foliage interest. In summer, it has attractive golden stripes down the margins of its long arching leaves. During late autumn or early winter, the leaves gradually turn to a striking orange-brown. It is a creeping grass that will spread out invasively unless kept in check. Increase by division in spring.

2m / 2m+

STIPA GIGANTEA
GOLDEN OATS
POACEAE

This a is a grass with tall arching flower stems, on which the flowers and seeds look particularly good against the sun. The attractive seeds last well into the winter. The low-growing evergreen narrow leaves are relatively unimportant visually. It grows on the banks beside water. Increase by division in spring.

2.5m / 2m

| height and spread | feature of interest | season of interest | *BOG/WATER GRASSES* **A – S** |

SHRUBS AND TREES

ACER SACCHARUM
SUGAR MAPLE
ACERACEAE

This will eventually become a large tree, so it is not for the small garden unless it is regularly replaced. The beauty of it comes when it produces some of the best of all autumn tints, and it should be positioned so that this colour reflects in the water. *A. palmatum* would be a better choice for smaller gardens.

ALNUS CORDATA
ITALIAN ALDER
BETULACEAE

Italian alder will eventually make a large tree. It likes wet conditions, and is particularly attractive when planted next to water. It has dark green shiny oval foliage that turns yellow in autumn. In spring it has attractive yellow catkins. Dark brown cones, produced in autumn, remain throughout winter.

ALNUS INCANA
GREY ALDER
BETULACEAE

An alder that may eventually grow big, but can be cut back to regenerate. It has dark green oval leaves that are grey underneath, and turn a fine yellow in autumn. Black catkins appear in autumn, and open to yellow in spring. Fruiting cones also appear in autumn and stay throughout the winter.

BETULA NIGRA
RIVER BIRCH
BETULACEAE

As its common name suggests, this a good birch for wet ground and one of the best for a bog garden. It has attractive shaggy bark that is pinkish-brown when young and reddish-black when older. The glossy green leaves turn yellow in autumn. It also produces yellow catkins in spring.

BETULA PENDULA
SILVER BIRCH
BETULACEAE

A graceful tree that looks good growing beside water, but should not be waterlogged. It will eventually grow big, but this may take many years and it can be replaced if necessary. Apart from its general shape, the main attraction is its white bark. It has catkins in spring and tints well in autumn.

CLETHRA ALNIFOLIA
SWEET PEPPER BUSH
CLETHRACEAE

This is a very hardy shrub that thrives in moist ground and is useful for a large bog garden. It is slow-growing but will eventually make a substantial bush, especially as it spreads by suckers. It has spikes of white fragrant flowers in late summer and takes on yellow autumn tints.

 leaf type   light preference   speed of growth   ease of growth

CORNUS ALBA 'SIBIRICA'
RED-BARKED DOGWOOD
CORNACEAE

Many of the *Cornus alba* cultivars are worth growing, especially as they do well on waterlogged soils. 'Sibirica' is particularly worthwhile for its red stems that are especially noticeable during the winter months. It should be cut back hard in spring to produce new growth for the following winter.

CORNUS STOLONIFERA 'FLAVIRAMEA'
YELLOW-STEMMED DOGWOOD
CORNACEAE

This is another shrub for winter, when its bright yellowish-green stems are at their best. They make a good contrast with the red stems of *C. alba* 'Sibirica'. Clusters of small white flowers appear on the older wood, but in order to get the best coloured bark it should be cut to the ground every spring.

HYDRANGEA MACROPHYLLA
MOPHEAD HYDRANGEA
HYDRANGEACEAE

Although thought of as general garden plants, hydrangeas do best in the moist conditions that a bog garden offers. There is a wide range of species and cultivars that can be considered, but the mophead hydrangeas are some of the most popular and easiest to grow. The flowers are red, blue or white.

KALMIA LATIFOLIA
CALICO BUSH
ERICACEAE

All kalmias like a deep rich moist soil, but they dislike alkaline conditions. The calico bush is a delightful shrub when in flower, when it produces masses of saucer-shaped blooms carried in clusters. The flowers are a soft pink colour and are attractive in bud as well as in bloom.

LIQUIDAMBAR STYRACIFLUA
SWEET GUM
HAMAMELIDACEAE

This is a tree that is distinguished by its exceptional autumn foliage, when it turns a deep red. Such foliage looks marvellous when seen across water. Unfortunately, given time it will become a large tree and so is not suitable for the smaller garden unless replaced once it begins to get too big.

METASEQUOIA GLYPTOSTROBOIDES
DAWN REDWOOD
TAXODIACEAE

A tall coniferous tree with very soft light green foliage and a reddish-brown fibrous bark. It is deciduous and the leaves turn yellow in autumn. It will eventually grow very tall but it is an elegant conifer for planting near water if you have the space. The swamp cypress, *Taxodium distichum*, is similar.

⚊ height and spread   ✳ feature of interest   ▭▭▭ season of interest   *SHRUBS AND TREES* **A – M**

SHRUBS AND TREES

MYRICA GALE
BOG MYRTLE
MYRICACEAE

Bog myrtle often grows in waterlogged areas where few other shrubs will survive. It has brownish-yellow catkins that shine out in spring, and round dark reddish-green foliage which is noted for its fragrance. The bushes can form a considerable thicket, although it can be controlled.

POPULUS BALSAMIFERA
BALSAM POPLAR
SALICACEAE

These are fast-growing trees that will grow in boggy conditions. They make good quick screens, and are noted for the balsam-scented resin exuded from the buds and leaves. The leaves have the typical poplar shape and are fresh green. Their uptake of water is good for drying out areas that are too wet.

POPULUS TREMULA
ASPEN
SALICACEAE

The aspen is well known for the effect of its trembling leaves, which move in the slightest breeze. The leaves are grey-green on top and white underneath, that latter 'flashing' as the leaves tremble. Although it does not like waterlogged conditions, it prefers moist soil and is suitable for a position by a pond.

SALIX ALBA VAR. SERICEA
SILVER WILLOW
SALICACEAE

Also known as *S.a.* f. *argentea*, this is mainly grown for the incredible colour of its foliage, although it has good winter-coloured bark. Both sides of its narrow leaves are covered with hairs, giving them an intense silvery appearance. It can grow quite big but can be coppiced to make it suitable for a smaller garden.

SALIX ALBA SUBSP. VITELLINA 'BRITZENSIS'
SCARLET WILLOW
SALICACEAE

This can be left to develop into a tree, but it is usually coppiced annually either at ground level or on a short trunk so that it produces a new crop of stems each year. With this technique the stems stay a rich deep red and make an attractive winter feature. It is good for growing in a bog garden or beside a pond.

SALIX BABYLONICA
WEEPING WILLOW
SALICACEAE

Weeping willow must be one of the most stunning trees to grow next to water, with its pendulous branches sweeping down to the water's surface. However tempting it may seem, it does grow very large and has an extensive questing root system, both of which make it suitable only for large gardens.

🌿 leaf type   ⬤ light preference   ⚘ speed of growth   ✿ ease of growth

SALIX CAPREA 'KILMARNOCK'
KILMARNOCK WILLOW
SALICACEAE

Also known as *S.c.* var. *Pendula*, this is a much better weeping willow for the small garden than *S. babylonica*. It is a grafted tree and so does not increase in height. It has a different form than the true weeping willow and is not as graceful, but still makes a good plant with its rounded head and cascading branches.

SALIX GRACILISTYLA 'MELANOSTACHYS'
BLACK CATKIN WILLOW
SALICACEAE

The species produces beautiful silver catkins, but the cultivar 'Melanostachys' produces even more spectacular ones. These are black, opening to reveal red anthers, and are set off against purplish-brown stems. The flowers appear on naked stems before the leaves open. The leaves are bright darkish green.

SALIX HASTATA 'WEHRHAHNII'
SALICACEAE

This willow is grown mainly for its flowers. It produces masses of beautiful silver catkins that stand upright on the contrasting dark purplish stems. It grows well in wet soils, and is therefore ideal for a bog garden. Use several plants to create an attractive thicket. The leaves are slightly silverish, especially underneath.

SALIX PURPUREA
PURPLE OSIER
SALICACEAE

The best form of this plant is the weeping form 'Pendula'. This is ideal for the small garden as it rarely grows much above 3m (10ft). It has weeping branches that are purple when they are young. In can be left as an arching shrub or carefully clipped to make the shape into a perfect weeping umbrella.

VACCINIUM VITIS-IDAEA
COWBERRY
ERICACEAE

A low bush that spreads to form a tangled mat of ground cover in acid soils, especially in boggy areas. It is a good plant for a large bog garden. It has bell-shaped flowers that are white tinged with pink and appear in late summer, followed by round red edible fruits. Koralle Group is the best form, with large fruits.

WISTERIA SINENSIS
PAPILIONACEAE

Not a water plant as such, but a beautiful plant to grow over water so that the large pendulous heads of flowers seem to drip down towards it. The fragrant flowers appear in spring and early summer and are mauve or white. It is usually grown a as a climber, and can be trained over a bridge or other support.

⚊⊥ height and spread   ✳ feature of interest   ▭▭▭ season of interest   *SHRUBS AND TREES* **M – W**

GLOSSARY

ALPINE: A plant that in its natural mountain habitat grows above the uppermost limit of trees. More colloquially, plants that are suitable for rock gardens are called alpines.

ANNUAL: A plant that grows from seed, flowers and dies within the same year. Some half-hardy perennial plants are used as annuals, that is, they die off in the winter.

AQUATIC PLANT: A plant that lives totally or partly submerged in water.

AXIL: The upper angle between leaf and stem.

BEDDING PLANTS: Plants that are set out for a temporary seasonal displays and discarded at the end of the season.

BIENNIAL: A plant raised from seed that makes its initial growth in one year and flowers during the following one, then dies.

BOG GARDEN PLANTS: Plants that live with their roots in moist soil.

BULB: An underground food storage organ formed of fleshy, modified leaves that enclose a dormant shoot.

CALYX: The outer and protective part of a flower. It is usually green and is very apparent in roses.

COMPOST: Vegetable waste from kitchens, as well as soft parts of garden plants, which is encouraged to decompose and to form a material that can be dug into soil or used to create a mulch around plants.

CORM: An underground storage organ formed of a swollen stem base, for example, a gladiolus.

CULTIVAR: A shortened term for 'cultivated variety' that indicates a variety raised in cultivation. Strictly speaking, most modern varieties are cultivars, but the term variety is still widely used because it is familiar to most gardeners.

CUTTING: A section of plant which is detached and encouraged to form roots and stems to provide a new independent plant. Cuttings may be taken from roots, stems or leaves.

DEAD-HEADING: The removal of a faded flower head to prevent the formation of seeds and to encourage the development of further flowers.

DORMANT: When a plant is alive but is making no growth, it is called dormant. The dormant period is usually the winter.

EVERGREEN: Plants that appear to be green throughout the year and not to lose their leaves are called evergreen. In reality, however, they shed some of their leaves throughout the year, while producing others.

FRIABLE: Soil that is crumbly and light and easily worked. It especially applies to soil being prepared as a seedbed in spring.

HALF-HARDY: A plant that can withstand fairly low temperatures, but needs protection from frost.

HALF-HARDY ANNUAL: An annual that is sown in gentle warmth in a greenhouse in spring, the seedlings being transferred to wider spacings in pots or boxes. The plants are placed in a garden or container only when all risk of frost has passed.

HARDEN OFF: To gradually accustom plants to cooler conditions so that they can be planted outside.

HARDY: A plant that is able to survive outdoors in winter. In the case of some rock-garden plants, good drainage is essential to ensure their survival.

HERB: A plant that is grown for its aromatic qualities. Many herbs can be used in cooking or medicinally.

HERBACEOUS PERENNIAL: A plant with no woody tissue that lives for several years. Herbaceous perennials may be deciduous or evergreen.

HYBRID: A cross between two different species, varieties or genera of plants.

LOAM: Friable mixture of sand, silt and clay.

MARGINAL PLANTS: Plants that live in shallow water at the edges of ponds. Some also thrive in boggy soil surrounding a pond.

MULCHING: Covering the soil around plants with well-decayed organic material such as garden compost, peat or in the case of rock garden plants, stone chippings or 6mm (¼ in) shingle.

NEUTRAL: Soil that is neither acid nor alkaline, with a pH of 7.0, is said to be neutral. Most plants grow in a pH of about 6.5.

PEAT: A naturally occurring substance formed from partly rotted organic material in waterlogged soils, used as a growing medium and soil additive.

PERENNIAL: Any plant that lives for three or more years is called a perennial.

PERGOLA: An open timber structure made up of linked arches.

POTTING COMPOST: Traditionally, a compost formed of loam, sharp sand and peat, fertilizers and chalk. The ratio of the ingredients is altered according to whether the compost is used for sowing seeds, potting-up or repotting plants into larger containers. Recognition of the environmental importance of conserving peat beds has led to many modern composts being formed of other organic materials, such as coir or shredded bark.

PRICKING OUT: Transplanting seedlings from the container in which they were sown to one where they are more widely spaced.

RACEME: An elongated flower head with each flower having a stem.

RAISED BED: A raised area, that is encircled by a wall or other barrier. Rock garden plants can be grown both in the raised bed and the wall.

RHIZOME: An underground or partly buried horizontal stem. They can be slender or fleshy. Some irises have thick, fleshy rhizomes, while those of lily-of-the-valley are slender and creeping. They act as storage organs and perpetuate plants from one season to another.

SEED LEAVES: The first leaves that develop on a seedling, which are coarser and more robust than the true leaves.

SEMI-EVERGREEN: A plant that may keep some or all of its leaves in a reasonably mild winter.

SINK GARDENS: Old stone sinks partly filled with drainage material and then with freely draining compost. They are planted with miniature conifers and bulbs, as well as small rock garden plants. These features are usually displayed on terraces and patios.

SPECIES ROSE: A common term for a wild rose or a near relative of it.

STAMEN: The male part of a flower.

STANDARD: A tree or shrub trained to form a rounded head of branches at the top of a clear stem.

SUB-SHRUB: Small and spreading shrub with a woody base. It differs from normal shrubs in that when grown in temperate regions its upper stems and shoots die back during winter.

TENDER: A plant which will not tolerate temperatures below freezing is referred to as tender.

TOPSOIL: The uppermost layer of soil which is structured and contains organic matter and humus.

TUBER: A swollen, thickened and fleshy stem or root. Some tubers are swollen roots (dahlia), while others are swollen stems (potato). They serve as storage organs and help to perpetuate plants from one season to another.

TURION: A winter bud that develops on some aquatic plants, drops to the floor of the pond in autumn and reshoots in spring.

VARIEGATED: Usually applied to leaves and used to describe a state of having two or more colours.

VARIETY: A naturally occurring variation of a species that retains its characteristics when propagated. The term is often used for cultivars.

WILDLIFE POND: An informal pond, often positioned towards the far end of a garden, which encourages the presence of wildlife such as frogs, birds, insects and small mammals.

INDEX

ACKNOWLEDGEMENTS

t *top* **b** *below* **l** *left* **r** *right* **Directory a–f**, *starting from top*

A-Z Botanical Collection 69b, 100a / Christian Martin Bahr 66f / Michael Chandler 74c/ Greg Kosteria 73d / Roy Lacey 86f / G Matthew 105f / F Merlet 65e, 67b / Helmut Partsch 81a / Dan Sams 64a / Margaret Sixsmith 65c / Roger Standen 65f / Archie Young 77d;

Deni Bown 78b;

Bruce Coleman Collection / Jane Burton 34l, 35l / Eric Crichton 34r / Felix Labhardt 107d / Hans Reinhard 35r;

Liz Eddison 2 & 45, 14b, 18b, 20t, 22, 26, 30l, 32l, 33r, 50, 66d, 68e, 69c, 78e / Natural & Oriental Water Garden 4 & 33l, 7 & 112, 10-11, 12, 15, 18t, 31r, / Alan Sargent, Chelsea '99 30r;

The Garden Picture Library / David Cavagnaro 68d / John Glover 100d / Sunnvia Harte 83b / Jerry Pavia 100c / John Ferro Sims 101d / Ron Sutherland 80a, 92f;

Garden & Wildlife Matters 67f;

John Glover 6, 13, 15t,b, 16, 19, 20b, 28–29, 31l, 36, 38, 47, 52, 55, 57, 58, 60–61 / Julian Dowle, Chelsea '97 1 & 32r / Dennis Fairweather 48 / Fiona Lawrenson, Chelsea '97 14t / Natural & Oriental Water Garden 40 / Pots & Pithoi 5 / Peter Styles, Chelsea '96 24 / Geoff Whiten, Chelsea '96 21;

Andrew Lawson 82d, 103b;

Peter McHoy 65a,b,d, 66a,e, 67a,d,e, 69f, 70b,c, 71b, 72b,f, 73a,b, 74b, 75a,d,e, 76d,e, 77a,b, 78d, 79d,f, 80b,e,f, 81e, 82c,e, 83d, 84c,d, 85c, 87c,d,e, 88b, 89e, 90e,f, 91a,b,d, 92b, 93d,e, 98b, 99a,d, 100f, 102b,c,f, 103a, 104c,f, 105a, 107c,e,f;

Oxford Scientific Films / Stephen Dalton 64c,f / Terry Heathcote 77f;

The Harry Smith Collection 64b,d,e, 66b,c, 68a,b,c,f, 69a,d,e, 70a,d,e, 71a,c,d,e,f, 72a,c,d,e, 73c,e,f, 74a,d,e,f, 75b,c,f, 76a,b,c,f, 77c,e, 78a,c,f, 79a,c, 80c,d, 81b,c,d,f, 82a,b,f, 83a,c,f, 84a,b,e,f, 85a,b,e,f, 86a,b,c,d,e, 87b,f, 88a,c,d,e,f, 89b,c,d,f, 90a,b,c,d, 91c,e,f, 92a,c,d,e, 93a,b,c,f, 94a,b,c,d,e,f, 95a,b,c,d,e,f, 96a,b,c,d,e,f, 97b,c,d,e,f, 98a,d,e,f, 99b,c,e,f, 100b,e, 101a,b,c,f, 102a,d,e, 103c,d,e,f, 104a,b,d,e, 105b,c,e, 106a,b,c,d,e,f, 107a,b;

David Squire 79e, 83e, 85d, 87a, 89a, 97a, 98c, 105d;

Stapeley Water Gardens Ltd 70d, 79b.